Praise for *On Teaching Science*

On Teaching Science provides a masterful "back to basics" review of true "nuts and bolts" of learning and teaching science. Author Jeffrey Bennett skillfully blends a modern view of the nature of science with insights into student learning, forming a "how-to" manual that would be of good use to any teacher of science, kindergarten through university level. Dr. Bennett takes on the American cultural rise of multitasking, inadequate study habits, and emphasis on unconnected knowledge tidbits. He builds a case for focused study and conceptual learning orchestrated by teachers who model enthusiasm, curiosity, creativity, and hard work. Science teachers at all levels of experience should read this book and rethink how they operate in the classroom and how they set expectations for students.

> — Dr. Alan McCormack, Professor of Science Education, San Diego State University, and President of the National Science Teachers Association (2010–11)

Success = more (and more efficient) study time. With this simple yet powerful formula, *On Teaching Science* is poised to change the national conversation about educational reform. Bennett compellingly argues that educational reforms should be evaluated by whether they increase student effort and study time (and not of the "check-the-box" kind but the type that requires applying one's mind). This approach would not only improve students' academic outcomes but have long-term consequences for the future of our democracy in which citizens need to contend with issues of increasing complexity.

> — Dr. Josipa Roksa, Associate Professor of Sociology and Education, University of Virginia, and co-author of *Academically Adrift* (U. Chicago Press, 2011)

Far and away the best book about teaching I've ever read. Beyond just the teaching of science, this book is a must read for every teacher, parent, administrator, and even student. *On Teaching Science* will be the gold standard to which all other teaching books will be compared in the future.

> — Brad A. Shonk, 4th Grade Teacher, 2010 Mississippi Teacher of the Year

On Teaching Science is GREAT. It should be required reading for parents and administrators as well as teachers.

> — Dr. Laura L. Duncan, Science Teacher, Boulder High School

A wonderful book, full of useful lessons not just about teaching science, but about teaching and learning in general.

> — Dr. Scott Hildreth, Professor of Physics and Astronomy, Chabot College

Dr. Bennett provides both experienced and novice teachers with reflective tools and specific strategies that will help us all improve our instruction and ensure student success. *On Teaching Science* should be required reading for teachers of all subjects at all levels, not just teachers of science.

> — Mark Levy, Adjunct Associate Professor of Education, St. Johns University

Bennett directs our attention to the importance of teaching in context and offers rich examples of how that might be accomplished. Even after 35 years in the classroom, I still found new ideas that I can use every day, as well as numerous ideas that will help educators seeking to implement the Next Generation Science Standards.

> — Bob Feurer, High School Science Teacher, 2011 Nebraska Teacher of the Year

Filled with insights into how to teach effectively with a truly positive undertone, *On Teaching Science* also shows how to open students' minds so that they will *want* to learn and will understand the true lifelong impacts of education. A must-read for new and seasoned teachers and professors alike, and a book I wish I'd been able to read before I started teaching. — Dr. Susan Lederer, Professor of Physics, California State University, San Bernardino, and NASA Johnson Space Center

Antoine de Saint-Exupéry proclaimed "If you want to build a ship, don't drum up people to collect wood and don't assign them tasks and work, but rather teach them to long for the endless immensity of the sea." *On Teaching Science* shows how to kindle in students that longing to learn about their universe and how to keep them engaged all the way along their journey to science. — Alvin Drew, NASA Astronaut (STS-118, STS-133)

On Teaching Science is packed with insights on education and how students learn that will make anyone a better teacher. Bennett provides practical steps that can be brought into the classroom at any level to improve student learning.
— Dr. Josh Colwell, Professor of Astrophysics, University of Central Florida

On Teaching Science is a valuable resource for anyone teaching or planning to teach science on the K–12 and college levels. It is a practical, concise guide to teaching in general, and to teaching science in particular, that will also ultimately lead to a greater understanding of science for students of all ages.
— John DiElsi, Dean of Online Learning, Mercy College

Bennett does a great job of distilling what it means to be a great science teacher into a manageable number of big ideas, teaching suggestions, and strategies, applied to both K–12 and higher education. I recommend *On Teaching Science* to all science teachers — it will support the good things you are already doing and provide ideas for how to do better.
— Lauren Monowar-Jones, Ohio Department of Education, Performance Assessment

Most of us recall our science classes as low-grade theater, in which an earnest teacher would spend an hour each day trying to ladle facts and ideas into our marginally absorbent brains. In *On Teaching Science*, Jeffrey Bennett steps back and sees what's really going on in education. His insights can fine tune this process, and turn a lumbering old Chevy into a Maserati. Time spent with his book can — as they say — change the world.
— Dr. Seth Shostak, Senior Astronomer, SETI Institute

On Teaching Science provides such a great refresher of key teaching principles that I'd recommend every teacher reread it at least once every five years. It will always help you refocus your efforts as you teach today's children.
— Debbie Biggs, STEM Teacher Leader, Clarke County Public Schools

Every education college/department should make *On Teaching Science* a required reading for teachers. It is fantastic! — Patricia Tribe, CEO, Story Time From Space, and former Director of Education for Space Center Houston

Additional reviews posted at OnTeachingScience.com

On Teaching Science

Principles and Strategies That
Every Educator Should Know

Also by Jeffrey Bennett

For Children

Max Goes to the Moon

Max Goes to Mars

Max Goes to Jupiter

Max Goes to the Space Station

The Wizard Who Saved the World

For Grownups

Beyond UFOs: The Search for Extraterrestrial Life and Its Astonishing Implications for Our Future

Math for Life: Crucial Ideas You Didn't Learn in School

What Is Relativity? An Intuitive Introduction to Einstein's Ideas, and Why They Matter

High School/College Textbooks

Using and Understanding Mathematics: A Quantitative Reasoning Approach

Statistical Reasoning for Everyday Life

Life in the Universe

The Cosmic Perspective

The Essential Cosmic Perspective

The Cosmic Perspective Fundamentals

On Teaching Science

Principles and Strategies That
Every Educator Should Know

Jeffrey Bennett

Big Kid Science
Boulder, CO
Education, Perspective, and Inspiration for People of All Ages

Published by
Big Kid Science
Boulder, CO
www.BigKidScience.com
Education, Perspective, and Inspiration for People of All Ages

Book web site: **www.OnTeachingScience.com**

Distributed by IPG
Order online at www.ipgbook.com
or toll-free at 800-888-4741

Editing: Joan Marsh, Lynn Golbetz
Composition and design: Side By Side Studios

Figures 3, 4, 5, and Excerpt Figure 2.2 adapted from Bennett, Jeffrey, Donahue, Megan, Schneider, Nicholas, and Voit, Mark, *The Cosmic Perspective*, 7th edition (2014). Printed and electronically reproduced by permission of Pearson Education, Inc., Upper Saddle River, New Jersey.

ISBN: 978-1-937548-40-7

Table of Contents

6 Seven Pedagogical Strategies for Success in Science Teaching   65

7 Putting It All Together   105

Introduction

Human history becomes more and more
a race between education and catastrophe.
— H. G. Wells

If you haven't already done so, I hope you'll take a moment to read the quote from H. G. Wells above. Think about what it means to you, both as a person and as an educator. I've chosen to open with this quote because I suspect that it will ring true to anyone involved in education, and especially to those in science education. Science and technology have put vast power into our hands, but with power comes responsibility, and responsibility requires understanding. I believe that many of the most serious challenges to our survival as a civilization stem from the fact that so many people, including far too many policy makers, do not understand the challenges well enough to face them wisely. As teachers and educators — and this latter category includes not only those making education a career, but also parents, community leaders, and students who are considering teaching as a career — our most important job is to change this dynamic, so that we as a civilization can successfully understand and address the many challenges to our future.

Of course, we have many other jobs as well. At the same time that we must educate the broader public, we must also train the next generation of experts and innovators. With younger children, whether our own or those we teach, we need to provide the inspiration that will make them want to learn enough so that they can make their own contributions to a better future. As students get older, we must provide them with the preparation they need to move along to each next step in achieving their long-term goals. In high school that means preparing students for college, while also making sure that those who don't go to college still learn enough to participate as educated citizens in our democracy. In college, it means preparing students for the coursework that will follow in their major courses, along with teaching them the practices they'll need for their careers, while at the same time giving them the critical reasoning skills that they will need to succeed in the modern world.

The good news is that, despite the wide variety of settings in which we may work, I believe that a few simple ideas can help all of us become better teachers. This short book is my attempt to summarize these ideas in a way that will (hopefully) make it easy for you to apply them in your own work. Please note that this is *not* a book based on the latest educational research; indeed, as I'll discuss later, most of what I'll be telling you has been known and practiced by great teachers for thousands of years. Nor is this book designed to tell you how to teach your specific subject matter, or to provide you with specific activities or resources. Rather, my aim is simply to offer a few general reminders of principles that you've probably thought about before and that are crucial to student learning, in hopes that by thinking about them again, we'll all be able to make a greater contribution to winning the race between education and catastrophe.

Because this book is meant to be a relatively short set of useful ideas, it could in principle be organized in many different ways. I've settled on an approach that I hope will make the ideas a little easier to remember, which is to use a sequence of odd numbers for my major topic areas, as follows:

- After a brief discussion of the definition of teaching and the nature of science, I'll focus on what I believe to be the ONE key to student success.
- Next, I'll present what I call THREE big picture ideas about teaching.
- Then we'll turn to FIVE general suggestions on how to be a successful teacher.
- Finally, I'll offer SEVEN more specific pedagogical strategies that I believe can help in any teaching, but especially in the teaching of science and math.

This book is adapted and expanded from a talk I've given primarily to college faculty and most commonly to faculty teaching astronomy or physics. As a result, most of my examples are drawn from those areas. Nevertheless, I will try to keep the examples general enough so that you'll be able see how similar examples could apply to your own teaching. Special notes call out ideas that might apply more specifically to particular educational levels or subjects. I therefore hope that you'll be able to adapt these ideas to your own teaching, no matter what grade level or subject area you happen to be teaching.

Please also note that while most of my specific suggestions are aimed at those readers who teach courses in science (or the other so-called STEM fields: science, technology, engineering, and mathematics), I hope that the general discussion will be of interest to readers who are involved with science teaching more indirectly, including parents, school administrators, policy makers, community leaders, and research scientists. Indeed, I hold out at least some small hope that the ideas in this book will help contribute to the national conversation about education by helping readers think about the challenges we must meet in order to improve our educational system.

On a final introductory note, I have created a web site for this book, OnTeachingScience.com. I'm cautiously optimistic that I'll find a way to make this an interactive site, where you will be able to post your own comments or additional suggestions to accompany those I've offered in this book. Please visit the site to see if it is useful to you.

With that, it's time to begin. I hope you will find the short time needed to read this book to be time well spent.

What Is Teaching?

If you're going to be a teacher, a good starting point is to have a working definition of what it means to teach. This is harder than it sounds. If you look in a dictionary, you'll find a number of alternate ways of defining the word *teach*, most of which boil down in one way or other to something along the lines of "to impart knowledge." But this is clearly inadequate as either a definition or a goal for teaching, because if all we did was impart knowledge, then each generation would learn only what the previous generation imparted to them; in other words, our civilization would never advance. So I'll offer you what I believe to be a better working definition:

> **Teaching** The transmission from one person to others of knowledge *and* of the means to acquire additional knowledge.

It's the second part of this definition that presents the greater challenge. Any good storyteller can transmit knowledge to an audience, but a teacher must also inspire the members of an audience to create their own, new stories. Indeed, while any particular course will focus on some specific set of subject matter, I'd argue that our primary goal in teaching is less for students to remember the particulars of a course than for them to "learn how to learn," so that they'll be successful in future endeavors.

It's worth noting that this definition of teaching poses a measurement problem, because it means that true success in teaching can be measured only by evaluating the long-term success of your students, meaning their success long after they've left your course. In essence, the assignments and exams that we can grade in the short term can at best tell us only some reasonable probability as to whether we've been successful teachers. This measurement problem should not stop us from trying to evaluate teaching success, but it means we must be careful to recognize the limitations of any evaluations that we use.

What Is Science?

Since this book focuses on the teaching of science, it would be useful to know exactly what *science* is. It's not easy to define science in a concise way; indeed, scholars who investigate the history and nature of science do not always agree on exactly what constitutes science. Nevertheless, it's clearly critical that we help students understand the basic nature of science and of how to distinguish science from nonscience, so I'll offer an approach that I've found to be successful with a variety of audiences. This approach begins by focusing on the purposes of science and then discusses key hallmarks that can help us distinguish between science and other methods of seeking knowledge.

Purposes of Science: One of the first problems we encounter in teaching science is that most students don't have a clear idea of the value of science. In many cases, students come to us with great misconceptions about the role of science in society; some even believe, for example, that the purpose of science is to undermine religion or other personal beliefs. I therefore find it effective to begin any discussion of the nature of science with what I believe to be three important purposes of science in society:

1. *Science is a way of distinguishing possibilities from realities.*
   This statement represents the idea that in the absence of evidence, we can imagine a broad range of possible explanations for any set of phenomena. Science gives us a way to look at evidence that can allow us to determine which of those possibilities are consistent with observed reality and which are not. The classic example is the ancient debate over whether Earth is the center of the universe or a planet going around the Sun. For more than 2,000 years, the debate over the two possibilities continued almost without change — and with most people believing the possibility that turned out to be incorrect — because observations were not yet precise enough to test whether one idea

offered a better match to reality than the other. Then, as observations improved during the Copernican revolution, we ultimately learned that the Earth-centered possibility simply did not agree with the evidence. Perhaps equally significant, nearly everyone supporting the alternate possibility had assumed that planetary orbits would be circular, but the data showed that this was also inconsistent with the evidence. That is what led Kepler to investigate other possibilities, enabling him to discover that Earth and other planets follow elliptical orbits around the Sun. For a simple bottom line, without science, we would likely still live in a world in which most people thought Earth to be the center of the universe.

2. *Science is a way of helping people come to agreement.*
   This statement simply reminds us of the way science advances. We collect evidence that anyone can in principle examine, and we analyze the evidence to decide what it means. We then put our conclusions to the test by looking at what our ideas predict about what we should find in other observations or experiments. If the predictions fail, then we know we have to go back to the drawing board. But if the predictions are verified, then we think our ideas are on the right track and we can build a model of nature based on them. If the model succeeds repeatedly and in varied circumstances, then the evidence can eventually become so overwhelming that anyone who looks at it will reach the conclusion that the model is valid. Again, the Copernican revolution provides a classic example. The debate about whether Earth was the center of the universe went on for more than 2,000 years. Then, over a period of barely more than a century, the evidence became so overwhelming that virtually no one argued any further for the Earth-centered view. Stated slightly differently, it's possible to argue endlessly as long as there are no actual facts to get in the way — and only science brings us the facts and understanding that can ultimately settle the debates.

3. *Science is the primary driver of technological progress.*
   Our society has undergone tremendous technological change in the past few centuries, and while there is room for debate on whether these changes have been a net positive or negative for the human race, there are very few people who advocate halting our technological progress. However, strange as it may seem to those of us who teach science, many people don't recognize the fact that science drives tech-

nology. For example, while nearly everyone favors advances in medical treatment, far fewer understand that these advances are connected to fundamental biology (including being rooted in an understanding of the theory of evolution). This type of misunderstanding often leads to debates about the value of fundamental research, putting at risk the very types of scientific investments that are necessary to continue technological progress. Only by connecting science and technology can we show people the intimate and important role that science plays in our everyday lives.

By emphasizing these three purposes, I've found that we can often overcome the misgivings of many of those who question the value of science. After all, who can be against something that helps us learn about reality, that brings people to agreement, and that is responsible for the technology that we have come to depend on?

Hallmarks of Science: In addition to helping people understand the value of science, we must also help them understand how science actually works. To this end, I find it useful to emphasize that science begins with careful observations of the world around us, and then to offer a set of three concrete "hallmarks of science"[1] that can be used by both students and the public to distinguish between science and nonscience:

1. **Modern science seeks explanations for observed phenomena that rely solely on natural causes.**

2. **Science progresses through the creation and testing of models of nature that explain the observations as simply as possible.**

3. **A scientific model must make testable predictions about natural phenomena that would force us to revise or abandon the model if the predictions do not agree with observations.**

These hallmarks may not be foolproof, but I believe that they are solid enough to allow students to look at claims and decide for themselves whether those claims are scientific in nature. (For more detail on the hallmarks and other ideas about the nature of science, please see "Excerpt 1: What Makes It Science?" starting on page 123.)

---

[1] Many people have contributed to the current wording of these hallmarks, but credit goes especially to several of my textbook co-authors: Mark Voit, Megan Donahue, Nick Schneider, Seth Shostak, and Bruce Jakosky.

NOTE: THE SCIENTIFIC METHOD You'll notice that the above description of science does not refer to the "scientific method," in which science is claimed to progress through a straightforward process of developing and testing hypotheses. The reason is simple: While the scientific method can be a useful idealization, the reality is that science rarely works this way. For example, Galileo did not point his telescope toward the heavens to test some particular hypothesis; he did it to see what he would see. Although it can be helpful for students (especially younger children) to apply the idealized scientific method to simple projects and experiments, we should be careful to emphasize that real science is much more creative, interesting, and fun.

NOTE: CREATIVITY AND SCIENCE As the above note reminds us, real science requires a high level of creative thinking. Unfortunately, this fact is not well known to many students and members of the general public, who tend to think of science (and especially of mathematics) as being the opposite of the creative arts. It's therefore very helpful to emphasize the creativity required in science, and worth noting that many scientists also excel in art, music, writing, and other creative endeavors. Indeed, making this connection may help encourage some young students who love the arts to realize that their creative talents also make them well suited to future careers in science.

Dealing with Creationism and Other Nonscientific Beliefs: Part of the reason that it is so important to talk about the nature of science is that we live in a society in which science is greatly misunderstood. As a result, we will encounter students and members of the public who hold a variety of nonscientific beliefs — such as beliefs in creationism (or intelligent design), UFOs, or parapsychology — and who in some cases may feel that the teaching of science is a threat to them. You can find many resources to help you with such situations, but I have found that the most effective strategy is to be gracious and nonconfrontational about personal beliefs, even while remaining clear about the division between science and other forms of seeking knowledge or understanding. Indeed, I believe that much of the public debate is a result of a natural defensiveness that arises when people believe that science is challenging their personal faith. As a result, we can often defuse the debate by making clear that we're out to teach about science, not to force anyone to accept it. In particular, I've found that we can overcome most objections to things like the teaching of evolution by letting students (and the public) know the following:

- Science is a way of acquiring knowledge about the world around us, and as discussed above, it has proven enormously successful in driving technological progress. It is this great success that explains why we teach science in schools. Nevertheless, science is not necessarily the only way to acquire knowledge, and students who wish to reject the conclusions of science are free to do so. The only thing we ask is that while they are in science class, they learn how science approaches and seeks to answer questions about the world.

- Just because something is nonscientific does not make it wrong. Consider UFO sightings: Because many of them have not been conclusively identified, it remains possible that people have witnessed alien spacecraft visiting Earth. The reason we don't teach about this topic in science classes is that it does not involve the type of evidence that allows us to investigate the topic scientifically; that is, it does not meet the three hallmarks of science.

- Science says nothing at all about the existence or nonexistence of God or any other form of the supernatural. That is because the supernatural by definition falls outside the realm of the hallmarks of science. For this reason, science should not be a threat to anyone.

- In accord with its second purpose (see page 4), science always seeks to help people come to agreement. When there are significant disagreements about the science of an issue, it generally means the evidence is not yet strong enough to support clear conclusions. When we call something a *scientific theory* — like the theory of gravity, the theory of the atom, the theory of relativity, and the theory of evolution — it means the evidence is so overwhelming that nearly everyone who has studied it in depth has come to agreement on the theory's validity. It is this unanimous or near-unanimous agreement that leads us to believe it deserves to be taught in the classroom, not any judgment call about personal opinions.

- Science is never finished. Every answer in science leads to new questions, and even the most successful theories still leave some questions unanswered. That is why, for example, scientists still ask questions about how evolution works, even though there is virtually unanimous scientific agreement on the general idea that life evolves over time by natural selection. Indeed, scientists are always looking for new questions to ask, because it is only by asking new questions that we can search for evidence and advance our scientific knowledge.

NOTE: TEACHING EVOLUTION The debate over the teaching of evolution is the most common one to arise with students and the public, and for that reason you can find an abundance of resources to help you with it. I especially recommend the judge's opinion from the 2005 *Dover* case (*Kitzmiller v. Dover Area School District*, 400 F. Supp. 2d 707 (M.D. Pa. 2005)), which is eloquently written and describes all the key issues. For something a bit shorter, I've included a second excerpt (Excerpt 2: Evolution in the Classroom, which begins on page 143) in which I have tried to give a concise summary of why evolution qualifies as science and should therefore be an integral part of the science curriculum, and of why alternative ideas such as creationism or intelligent design do not qualify as science.

NOTE: TEACHING ABOUT GLOBAL WARMING In recent years, the debate over teaching about global warming (climate change) has become nearly as contentious as the debate over evolution, especially since the Next Generation Science Standards emphasize the importance of the topic. Fortunately, this issue lacks the overtly religious implications of the debate over evolution, and I think the best defense of why we should teach it in school comes from the agreement issue (the second purpose of science above): Among scientists who have studied the evidence — which generally means climate scientists — there is extraordinary agreement on the basic science of the subject. (For a suggestion on how to approach the topic pedagogically, please see the discussion of climate science on pages 71–72.)

It's also worth noting an important practical difference between this debate and the debate over evolution: Fifty years from now, people who choose to reject evolution will still be just as free to do so as they are today. In contrast, unless we act rapidly to curtail greenhouse gas emissions, the models for global warming predict consequences within fifty years that will be impossible for anyone to ignore. In other words, the public debate over evolution is likely to continue for a very long time, but the debate over whether the world is warming is only temporary. (Of course, some may still claim it's a natural cycle rather than human caused, but the fact of warming will be abundantly clear.) In the meantime, even those who don't believe it should want to know what the scientists think, since that is the only way to gauge the level of risk we take if we choose to ignore the predicted consequences.

One Key to Student Success

I realize it may sound a bit audacious to claim that there's one key to all student success, but here it is:

Learning requires effort and study.

Having made this statement to many faculty audiences, I know that most of you are thinking, "Well, that's kind of obvious." After all, we all know that we have to work to learn anything, and learning complex ideas can require huge amounts of concentrated study time. I also know that a few of you may be preparing to argue the semantics, so I'll note that I'm using the term *study* in its broadest sense, which *Webster's Unabridged Dictionary* defines to be "application of the mind to the acquisition of knowledge." In that sense, "study" can apply to many different specific tasks, from intently listening to a teacher or reading a book to actively engaging in hands-on or group activities; it can even apply to a toddler learning to walk, since the mind must be applied to develop the necessary skills of coordination. So if we want students to succeed in our classes, we need to make sure they devote effort and study to the material we hope to teach them.

NOTE: WHAT COUNTS AS "STUDY" Be sure to pay attention to the first part of the definition of *study*: "application of the mind." It's quite possible to read a book or listen to a lecture without actually thinking about the material, in which case it's not truly study, but just an example of the old saying "in one ear and out the other." That is a major reason why science educators emphasize the importance of active engagement, such as hands-on activities. But even these are not foolproof, because it's also possible to be "in one hand and out the other" if the hands-on part can be done by rote or is formulaic, or if some members of a group can let others do the thinking for them. Time spent counts as "study time" only if students are really paying attention and reflecting on what they are doing.

The State of U.S. Education: As obvious as it ought to be, the importance of studying is too often forgotten. Indeed, as explained below, it is being forgotten throughout the U.S. education system today, to the great detriment of our students and society.

▶ **K–12 Education**: One of the great laments about U.S. education today is the way our students tend to underperform relative to their peers in other developed nations. While there are undoubtedly many reasons for this underperformance, I believe that one clear contributor is the well-documented fact that our students spend less time in school and less time studying outside of school. By the time they graduate high school, kids in many European and Asian nations have had the equivalent of one to two additional years of study time compared to American kids. Of course, simply adding more school time and more homework will not be a panacea, and if overdone it can even backfire. For example, I've had teachers from China tell me that their students are overworked to the point of stifling their creativity, and that they feel their kids would benefit from more free time to just "be kids." Nevertheless, given that study is the most important key to student success, we can't expect our students to do better unless we enable them to devote enough time to study. So while we must be careful not to overdo it — and as teachers we must work hard to make sure that any extra class time or study time will be time well spent (as opposed to "busy work") — a key factor in improving K–12 education will be more study time, whether that time comes in school, at home, in enrichment programs, or elsewhere.

NOTE: **STUDY EXPECTATIONS VARY GREATLY AMONG SCHOOLS** Please note that I'm talking about averages here, and you can certainly find cases in which schools or school districts appear to have gone overboard in the amount of work they expect from students, or in which much of the work is more tedious than useful. Nevertheless, on a national average basis, our problem is *too little* time for studying, not too much.

NOTE: **OPTIONS FOR INCREASING STUDY TIME** There are two general ways to increase study time: We can have our kids spend more time in school or we can have them do more work outside of school (or some combination of both). In principle, either option would be fine, but here's a practical reality: Today, kids from well-off families with well-educated parents almost universally get substantial academic help outside of school. At a minimum, they get help from their parents, and many get a variety of enrichment programs, great family trips, and other educationally beneficial experiences. In contrast, kids from poorer or less-educated families generally lack these opportunities; for example, research shows that for lower-income students, summer vacation is largely a time in which they forget what they've learned and fall even farther behind their peers. (For a great summary of the research on summer learning loss, see McCombs, J., et al., "Making Summer Count," RAND Education, 2011.)

Because of this reality, I believe the only equitable approach to education is to offer dramatically more school time — both more days per year and more hours per day. I realize that many well-off parents will object; perhaps there's a way to please everyone, such as by offering longer days and summer school as options rather than requirements. But one way or another, we must make sure that *all* kids have the time they need to study.

▶ **College Education**: I don't think there can be any more severe indictment of the state of college education today than is found in these recently reported statistics (Babcock, P., and Marks, M., "Leisure College, USA: The Decline in Student Study Time," *American Enterprise Institute Education Outlook*, no. 7, Aug. 2010):

- In the 1960s, full-time students spent an average of approximately 24 hours per week studying outside class.

- Today, full-time students spend an average of only about 14 hours per week studying outside class.

Unless students of today are somehow studying much more efficiently than students of the past—and given the distractions that students now face from their electronic devices, it's far more likely that the opposite is true—then this dramatic reduction in study time can only mean that college students today are learning much less than their counterparts of the past. In other words, by allowing this decline in study time, colleges are delivering less value to both students and society. If we do not find a way to reverse this trend, then college will increasingly become a waste of time and money for everyone involved.

NOTE: VALIDITY OF THE DECLINE CLAIM In case you are wondering whether these data might simply reflect the fact that more students today are juggling families and jobs along with school, I'll quote from the first page of the study by Babcock and Marks: "[T]he decline is not explained by changes over time in student work status, parental education, major choice, or the type of institution students attended." In other words, the authors claim that the comparison is between otherwise equivalent *full-time* students across the decades. The juggling acts of today's students may contribute to the pressures that have led to the decline in study time, but the conclusion that full-time students of today are studying less and therefore learning less than full-time students of the past still holds.

NOTE: THERE IS LESS DECLINE IN SCIENCE The news is not quite so bad for teachers of science: More detailed statistics (see Arum, R., and Roksa, J., *Academically Adrift*, University of Chicago Press, 2011) show that study time has declined less in science and other STEM (science, technology, engineering and mathematics) fields than in most other disciplines. Nevertheless, there is room for improvement, especially in classes at the introductory level. Although I have not found detailed data on this point, I believe that students *majoring* in science/STEM fields are generally studying as much or nearly as much as their peers did in the past; after all, the prerequisites for advanced science and engineering classes have not changed, and unless you understand the prerequisites you will not get far in subsequent classes. I therefore suspect that the decline in study time for science is coming from introductory-level classes, particularly those for nonscience majors, because these are the classes in which there is less pressure to ensure that students are prepared for higher-level coursework.

Indeed, the same idea likely explains the general college trend: Students majoring in STEM fields generally follow a course sequence in which each course builds upon previous courses; therefore, if a teacher of any one course fails to prepare students adequately, teachers in subsequent courses will quickly notice the deficiencies. In contrast, most non-STEM fields involve a series of courses that tend to be more individually distinct (that is, they don't rely so much on prerequisite knowledge), which means there is less pressure on teachers to ensure that their students learn a particular amount of material.

NOTE: REVERSING THE DECLINE TREND It's worth noting that while you as an individual teacher can help improve the situation in your own classes, the more general problem requires institutional reform. I suspect that anyone teaching at the college level can list numerous examples of pressure from students, parents, and the institutional reward system, which all conspire to push college faculty toward lowering expectations. After all, as my colleague Nick Schneider says, "College is the only business in which customers (students) often demand *less* for their money." If you really want to make an impact in improving college education, join with other faculty in finding ways to change the dynamics of these pressures. I won't pretend to have answers as to how best to accomplish this change, but clearly it must involve ensuring that the system rewards teachers who set the highest expectations and achieve the greatest student learning, which in most cases is very different from the way the reward system works today.

Multitasking: The many distractions that today's students face with their electronic devices brings up the more general issue of multitasking. In decades past, it was common to see students filling every available desk in a school's library, engaged in deep, concentrated study. Today, it is far more common for students to study while playing music, exchanging texts with friends, or watching YouTube videos. Like much of the general public — including many scientists and science teachers — these students believe that they are able to multitask successfully. In many cases, they even believe that the multitasking enables them to study more efficiently. Unfortunately, research shows that they are mistaken.

Numerous studies (for example, Ophir, E., Nass, C., and Wagner, A., "Cognitive control in media multitaskers," *Proceedings of the National Academy of Sciences*, 106, no. 37, Sept. 15, 2009) show not only that multitaskers perform more poorly than those who focus their attention on one task at a time, but also that those who believe they are best at multitasking actually tend to be the worst! The research is so clear that we should provide students with a new definition of multitasking:

Multitasking: Doing several things at once, all of them poorly

It won't be easy to convince all your students, but there's little doubt that we all do better when we focus on the task at hand without distractions.

The difficulty with multitasking means that in addition to spending less time studying than they should, students are probably absorbing even less than their study time might otherwise suggest. If we hope to improve education, we need to make sure not only that our students put in more study time but that they drop the multitasking in favor of concentrated effort.

One Key to Student Success

NOTE: TECHNOLOGY *CAN* BE BENEFICIAL While multitasking usually revolves around technology (cell phones, computers, etc.), the technology itself is not the problem. There are plenty of ways in which we can put technology to use in improving education, but they will be successful only if we also ensure that students still make a concentrated effort to study when using these technologies.

NOTE: DISTRACTED DRIVERS It's worth noting that the same issues that make multitasking inefficient for study make it downright dangerous for driving. I won't go into detail here, but research shows that if you talk on a cell phone, text, program your GPS, or have any other similar distractions while driving, you may be as dangerous as a drunk driver — and this is true even if you use your devices "hands free." Tell your students about this; you may save someone's life.

Consequences to Education — The Pressure to "Dumb Down": As previously noted, the fact that students are studying less automatically means that they are learning less, which in turn means that students will be unable to meet the same expectations that we had in the past. As a result, teachers and schools at all levels are forced to make a difficult choice: We either accept that students will do more poorly in our classes than students of the past, or we "dumb down" our expectations so that students can still meet them with their reduced study time. Because students, parents, and administrators all get very upset if we give lower grades, the institutional pressure ends up being to dumb down.

The pressure to lower expectations is so constant that it's easy to lose sight of it, but it has tended to create a vicious cycle of ever-lower workloads. For example, the fact that students are studying less tends to make us assign less to them. This, in turn, means that we cannot cover as much material in our courses, leading us to reduce both breadth and depth. The fact that our courses become less comprehensive means that teachers put pressure on administrators to lower their standards for students and on publishers to reduce the content in textbooks. Then, just when we might think students would be able to meet these newly lowered standards of success, the natural human inclination to try to work a little less takes us back to the beginning of the cycle, and the expectations fall further. The only way to break the cycle is to restore standards and restore expectations for study.

NOTE: THE COMMON CORE STANDARDS At the K–12 level, the most important effort to restore standards in at least the past half-century has been the development of the Common Core State Standards for mathematics and language arts, released in 2010, and the Next Generation Science Standards, released in 2013. The Common Core represents a bold effort to reverse the dumbing down of education and to raise the standards for learning. (For those who may not be familiar with its history, the Common Core effort was started by the National Governors Association in 2008, making it a bipartisan effort at curriculum reform driven from the state level.)

Unfortunately, the Common Core effort is now under attack, and several of the states that initially had committed to the Common Core have already removed themselves from the new standards. Part of the reason is political, as some groups see the Common Core effort as running contrary to the traditional "local control" of schools in the U.S. But another part simply has to do with pushback against higher expectations, as many parents and some teachers claim that the new standards are too much to ask of our students. For the sake of future generations, I encourage all of us to push for the acceptance of the Common Core, and then to work to meet its high expectations.

NOTE: DIGITAL TEXTBOOKS As a textbook author, I can't resist a note about the increasing use of digital resources in teaching, especially the move toward "digital textbooks." These digital resources can in principle offer great benefit to learning by, for example, providing video or animation to help explain complex concepts or by asking questions to check student understanding of key concepts before moving on to more advanced concepts. However, this promise can be realized only if two key principles are kept in mind:

1. Unless we want to encourage illiteracy in the next generation, digital resources such as video and interaction must be used as *enhancements* to reading, not as replacements for reading.

2. It is not yet clear that students can learn as effectively from e-books as from print books, and part of the reason is that e-books almost always mean attempting to study at the same time that you're getting texts, e-mails, Instagrams, etc.

So while we should certainly take advantage of the enhancements that digital resources can offer, I believe we should tread carefully in making a complete transition away from print books unless and until research demonstrates that students learn just as effectively from e-books. (For the programmers out there: How about creating an app that turns off all digital distractions except for access to the online resources being used for learning? I'd love to see a study that contrasts success at digital learning for students who use this app and those who don't.)

Consequences for Society: The immediate societal consequences of having students who don't study as much and learn as much are probably obvious: These students will be less able to compete in the global marketplace for jobs, which will hurt their own personal prospects while leaving the nation in a less competitive position. But I believe there is another major consequence that may be even more detrimental: Because so many of our citizens are able to get through school and get decent or good grades with so little work, they grow up to be adults who expect everything to come easily — which means they are not prepared to deal with the complexities of modern issues. Consider the national debt, tax policies, energy choices, global warming, or most any other major issue; all of these play a huge role in the way citizens vote today, yet they cannot be understood and thoughtfully addressed unless citizens put some reasonable amount of effort into studying them. When we have a population that expects things to come too easily, people end up making decisions based on sound bites or emotions, because they don't know how to put in the effort required to make decisions based on evidence and understanding.

Changing the National Conversation: In science, we know that it is easy to become overwhelmed if we focus solely on the vast body of facts and data that have been accumulated over time; that is why we instead focus on building an understanding of the underlying simplicity of nature, as expressed in comprehensive theories such as the theory of gravity, of the atom, or of evolution. I believe we should apply the same principle to education. For too long, we have allowed the national conversation about education to be fragmented into a series of small issues and Band-Aid reforms. This type of fragmented approach probably explains why educational improvement has been so difficult to achieve. After all, annual education spending exceeds $1 trillion per year in the United States alone, which means that even small changes are likely to harm someone's short-term financial interests and therefore to generate significant resistance. But there is an underlying simplicity to the idea that learning requires effort and study, and it provides a benchmark against which to judge any other proposed reforms:

If a reform promotes more (and/or more efficient) study time, then it is likely to be successful; if it doesn't, then it is likely to fail.

If this book accomplishes just one thing, I hope it will be to shift the national conversation about education to one that focuses primarily on the importance of study and hard work to success.

NOTE: AN EQUATION FOR SUCCESS I'll end this section with a wonderful "equation for success" that came from a remarkable source: Ugandan high school student Daniel Omoko, whom I was introduced to through the Educate! foundation (experienceeducate.org), which works with youth and education programs in Africa:

> *Hard work + Determination − Laziness = Success*
> — Daniel Omoko, Uganda

One Key to Student Success

Three Big Picture Ideas about Teaching

Let's return now to our working definition of teaching: The transmission from one person to others of knowledge *and* of the means to acquire additional knowledge. You'll notice that while this definition tells you what you are expected to accomplish as a teacher, it does not tell you how to do it. In fact, I do not believe that there is any simple formula that will always work. Teaching must be flexible, because every combination of subject matter and audience is unique. Nevertheless, I believe three "big picture ideas" about teaching are always useful to keep in mind.

Big Picture Idea 1

You can't actually "teach" anything to anybody; you can only help people learn for themselves.

In other words, a teacher's job is not to pour knowledge into students' heads, but to inspire and provide the tools for students to make the effort to study and learn for themselves. Or, as William Butler Yeats eloquently put it, "Education is not the filling of a pail, but the lighting of a fire."

Like most of the ideas we'll discuss, this one is fairly obvious once you think about it. (I recall one of my biochemistry professors once reminding our class of the importance of studying by telling us that "you don't learn by osmosis.") Yet we often seem to forget about its implications for teaching. We tend to judge teachers on characteristics that they themselves have, such as their dedication, their ability to manage their classrooms, or how well they can hold student attention as they speak and interact. I agree that most great teachers would score highly in all these characteristics, but I think we find a better way to define great teaching by combining our first big picture idea and our key to student success:

Great teachers provide their students with the inspiration and the tools needed to make the great effort of studying that is required to learn and to discover new things.

NOTE: THE IMPORTANCE OF MODELING BEHAVIORS FOR YOUR STUDENTS
Given the above definition of great teaching, the "hard part" of becoming a great teacher lies in figuring out how to provide your students with the inspiration and tools needed for effective study. Although there are no simple formulas for doing this, one clear characteristic of great teachers is that they *model the behaviors* that they would like their students to have. Modeling works because students will try to emulate teachers they respect and admire. In other words, if you want to be a great teacher, be sure you *show students your own enthusiasm, curiosity, creativity, and hard work*, so that they will see the value in developing similar behavioral patterns for themselves.

Big Picture Idea 2

Brains are brains. We may know more as we get older, but we still learn new things in the same basic way.

This idea might make a little more sense if I explain how it got on my list. When people find out that I write both college-level textbooks and children's books, they often ask me what it is like to write for "two such different audiences." But in fact, the audiences are not really all that different. I generally use the same techniques and strategies when I try to explain scientific concepts to the brightest college students as I do with primary-grade students; the only differences are that I can use higher-level vocabulary and assume more prior knowledge on the part of the older students.

The "brains are brains" idea also tells us that strategies for teaching that work for one group are likely to work for other groups as well. That is one reason why I'm hopeful that this book can be of use to teachers across a wide range of grade levels and science subject areas.

NOTE: "KNOWING" THINGS THAT ARE NOT TRUE It's important to realize that the fact that older students "know more" can cut both ways, because they often "know" things that are actually misconceptions. As an old saying goes,[2] "It ain't so much the things we don't know that get us into trouble, it's the things we know that just ain't so." This means that we often first have to help students unlearn their misconceptions (we'll discuss ways of doing this in Strategy 5) before we can hope to teach them correct scientific ideas.

An Example of "Brains Are Brains": As a case in point, I'll use the example that first led me to understand this second big picture idea. Early in my career, I ran a summer school focused on space science for kids entering grades 4 through 10. I quickly learned that all those beautiful NASA montages of planets and moons gave the students a very misleading picture, because it led them to imagine space as a place crowded with large worlds. I therefore created activities centered around building a scale model of the solar system on a 1-to-10 billion scale. (FYI, I chose that particular scale for three main reasons: (1) it falls within a rather narrow range of scales in which the planets are big enough to see while the distances between them are still walkable; (2) it makes the math easy enough for even elementary school kids to do for themselves, since they can look up real sizes and distances in metric units and then simply drop 10 zeros and convert prefixes as needed; and (3) on this scale, one light-year happens to equate to very nearly 1,000 kilometers, which makes it very easy to see how the same scale on which you can walk the solar system in a few minutes translates to the enormous distances to stars.)

Not long after, when I began teaching college astronomy, I found that the students came in knowing no more about scale than the elementary students (which really is not surprising, since the topic of scale is rarely taught at any level), and that I could best help them by using the very same scale activities that I had created for the elementary and middle school students. In fact, my own work on permanent scale model exhibits began with a set of my honors students at the University of Colorado, who did most of the legwork that led to the construction of the Colorado Scale Model Solar System on the Boulder campus, which in turn ultimately led to the creation of the *Voyage* Scale Model Solar System (Figure 1) on the National Mall in Wash-

---

[2] This quotation is often attributed to Mark Twain, but it clearly did not originate with him. In his book *The Quote Verifier* (2006), Ralph Keyes traces the original source to 19th-century humorist Josh Billings (1818–85).

Figure 1. This photo shows the pedestals housing the Sun (the gold sphere on the nearest pedestal) and the inner planets in the *Voyage* Scale Model Solar System in Washington, DC. The planets are encased in the sidewalk-facing disks visible at about eye level on the planet pedestals. The building at the left is the National Air and Space Museum. Other *Voyage* exhibits are located at Space Center Houston, in Kansas City, and in Corpus Christi, with more coming soon. Visit http://www.voyagesolarsystem.org/ for information on obtaining a *Voyage* exhibit for your own community (or send me an e-mail).

ington, DC (an effort directed and still run by Jeff Goldstein of the National Center for Earth and Space Science Education).

Perhaps the clearest illustration of the "brains are brains" idea came when we first took professional astronomers on walks through our scale model solar system. As they walked along and looked at how tiny the planets are in comparison to the distances between them, a typical reaction was an initial "That can't be right," followed by a pause in which they did the calculations in their heads and realized that the model was indeed correctly scaled. The point is that even for astronomers who spend entire careers studying this stuff, the visualization provided by an actual model helped them understand the concept of scale in a different way than they had understood it before.

NOTE: MORE ON VISUALIZATION As the scale model solar system example suggests, people of all ages benefit greatly from visualizations, which can make otherwise abstract ideas much more concrete. (See Strategy 4 for additional discussion of the importance of using concrete examples.) For this reason, it is always a good idea to try to come up with visualizations of what you are teaching, whether these are models, demonstrations, experiments, or relevant photos. As a brief illustration of this point, think about the photo of the *Voyage* scale model solar system (Figure 1): While the text discusses scale model solar systems in the abstract, the photo probably gives you a much more concrete idea of what I'm talking about. Moreover, the mere presence of the photo likely made more readers pay attention to this section than would otherwise have been the case. Students react similarly, which is why they will almost always learn better with visualizations than without them.

NOTE: NEARLY ALL SCIENTISTS CAN DO WELL SPEAKING TO CHILDREN For those of you who are professional scientists, I'd like to point out that the "brains are brains" idea means that you can help with one of our greatest national education problems, which is the fact that so few children ever get to meet or spend time with a "real" scientist. One reason for this fact is that while almost all professional scientists would be willing in principle to volunteer a small amount of time to work with young audiences, many are fearful that they wouldn't know what to do in such settings. The message of the "brains are brains" idea is that you should fear not. If you are able to teach your colleagues about your professional research, or to work successfully with graduate students, then teaching young children should come just as naturally; you'll just need to be sure that you adjust the level of your presentation appropriately (and most classroom teachers will help you do that if you meet with them for a few minutes before you meet with the students). That is, if you can inspire a graduate student, you can also inspire a third grader — and I hope that you will.

"Today's Students Learn Differently": You've probably heard it said that today's students learn differently than students of the past, which is said to be a result of the exposure they now have to technology and to vastly more information (at least as measured in bits and bytes) than students of the past. There's little doubt that the ubiquity of technology has changed the way that students interact with each other, with teachers, and with media; similarly, the fact that students now confront so much information on a daily basis means they need filtering skills that were not necessary in the past. Nevertheless, I'm highly skeptical of the claim that students *learn* in any different way. Although we don't know exactly how learning occurs, I don't think there can be any doubt that learning is a physiological process that involves biochemical changes in the brain. So the next time someone claims that today's students learn in some fundamentally different way, ask them how they think that brain physiology could have undergone a dramatic change in a single generation.

NOTE: OLD TEACHING STRATEGIES CAN STILL WORK An obvious corollary to the above idea is that teaching strategies that have successfully facilitated learning in the past should still be successful in the present. New methods and new technology may give us a means for reaching more students or for enhancing student understanding, but old methods can still be quite valuable.

NOTE: LEARNING AND AGE On a related note, I've been asked on occasion whether there is any detailed evidence to back my "brains are brains" claim that people of different ages learn in the same way. I'll answer in two ways. First, while as a scientist I think we should always seek evidence to back any claim, I'd argue that this particular one is at least somewhat self-evident. For example, it's hard to see how the basic physiology of building neural connections would change with age (though the speed and ease of the process might change), and experience shows that older learners need the same type of inspiration as younger learners before they'll make the effort to learn something new. That said, my second answer is that recent research does indeed seem to back the claim; see, for example, Garland, E., "Neuroplasticity, Psychosocial Genomics, and the Biopsychosocial Paradigm in the 21st Century," *Health Soc Work* 34, no. 3, Aug. 2009: 191–199.

Big Picture Idea 3

People have known how to teach successfully for thousands of years.

This fact explains why we have computers and cars and rockets while the ancient Egyptians did not. To see why, you just have to recognize that we are not inherently smarter than the ancient Egyptians (because the human brain has not evolved significantly since that time), so the fact that we know more and can do more means that people have been successfully transmitting knowledge and the means to acquire new knowledge from one generation to the next since that time.

Given how obvious this big picture idea may seem, you may wonder why I've bothered to put it on my list. One reason is that I believe it is important to keep a sense of humility about teaching and approaches to teaching. For example, while I'd be flattered if you thought I was providing you with new insights about teaching, the truth is that aside from the specific content examples, there's probably nothing that I can tell you about teaching that would have come as a great surprise to Plato, Aristotle, or Euclid. In fact, there's a wonderful quote often attributed to Euclid (though the attribution is almost certainly incorrect, a fact I verified with several noted historians of mathematics): "Most ideas about teaching are not new, but not everyone knows the old ideas."

The Art of Teaching: This third big picture idea also tells us that the teaching process is much more art than science. You can see this fact by considering the way we regard the works of great scientists and great artists of the past. The works of great artists are often just as great today as they were at the time of their creation, which is why people still pay to see original works of Michelangelo or of the ancient world. In contrast, appreciating the greatness of past works of science requires considering them in the context of their times. To put it a different way, we'd be very impressed by a modern student who created a sculpture like Michelangelo's *David*, but not so much by a student who replicated Galileo's observations of moons orbiting Jupiter. Teaching falls on the art side, because a great past teacher would still be great if we could transport him or her through time to today. (This also explains why we still read books written by great teachers of long ago.)

NOTE: THE ART OF TEACHING *CAN* BE STUDIED SCIENTIFICALLY The fact that teaching itself is an art does not in any way invalidate the scientific study of teaching. Just as we can study the techniques that make great artists successful, we can in principle use science to develop ways of evaluating the success of teaching and particular strategies of teaching. That, of course, is the goal of most educational research. (If you are not familiar with some of the great education research that is being done, a good place to start is at the Department of Education's Institute for Education Sciences, web link ies.ed.gov.)

Three Big Picture Ideas

Teaching Today: The most important reason why I've listed my third big picture idea is that it causes us to reflect on what is different about teaching today from teaching in the past, and the key difference is this:

- In the past, most teaching involved a close relationship between a teacher (mentor) and student, and often was one on one. As a result, real education was available to only a small fraction of the population.
- Today, we believe that everyone is entitled to education, which means that we need to "mass-produce" what used to be a limited experience.

It is this mass production of education that creates the major challenges of teaching today. When you teach one on one, you can generally tell whether your student is understanding and learning. But when you have 30 kids in third grade, or 200 students in a college lecture hall, or unseen students in an online course, it can be very difficult to determine how much learning is taking place.

In fact, I'll go so far as to suggest that virtually *all* of the difficulties we have in the education system today are a result of problems in our mass-production process. Therefore, the goal of any educational reform is not really to change teaching (which we've known how to do successfully for thousands of years), but rather to find better ways of mass-producing good teaching.

An analogy may help: The purpose and functionality of an automobile is the same no matter how it is made, but if you build them by hand, then only a few people will have them, while mass production makes them available to almost everyone. It's the same with teaching. No matter whether you teach one on one or to a large class, the goal of teaching is still to transmit knowledge and the means to acquire additional knowledge, and student success still depends on effort and study.

Five General Suggestions for Successful Teaching

If we consolidate the ideas we've discussed so far, your job as a teacher is to enable learning among as many of your students as possible. Because you cannot simply "pour" knowledge into students' heads, you must instead find ways to motivate them to learn for themselves. If you can do that for all of your course objectives while answering student questions clearly, accurately, and respectfully, then you will be a great teacher. With that in mind, I'll now offer five suggestions for successfully teaching in a mass-production setting.

General Teaching Suggestion 1

Above all, try to ensure that your students study.

This first suggestion is just a reiteration of the fact that studying is the key to student success, but it is so important that it has to be at the top of any list of successful teaching practices. Indeed, I would argue that the following two statements are both undeniable realities:

- You could be the world's best teacher, using the world's best teaching materials in the best possible ways, but if your students don't put in enough time studying, they still will not succeed in learning.
- Conversely, you could be a terrible teacher with terrible practices, but if your students go out and study enough on their own, they can overcome your deficiencies and succeed.

In other words, teaching success depends primarily on motivating students to put in the effort necessary for them to succeed.

That's really all there is to this first general teaching suggestion, but let's explore some of the issues involved in putting it into practice.

Time on Task: The first step in getting your students to study sufficiently is to have some sense of how much total "time on task" you should expect from them. By "time on task," I mean the total amount of time that a student devotes to your course material, including class time and all study time outside of class. Expectations for time on task vary with grade level; I'll start with college, for which there has long been a general consensus on the appropriate expectation.

▶ **College Education:** The traditional expectation in college study is expressed by the old rule of thumb that college students should spend about 2 to 3 hours studying outside class for each hour in class (or unit of credit). For example, for a 3-credit class that meets 3 hours per week, students should be putting in 6 to 9 hours per week of outside study.

You can see that this rule of thumb makes at least some sense by looking at the simple math that it implies for a college workload: If we assume that a full-time college load is 12 hours in class per week, then the rule of thumb suggests an additional 24 to 36 hours of study, for a weekly total of 36 to 48 hours of school work. This puts the expected time commitment of a full-time college student right in line with the typical expectation of a full-time job — which is as it should be. Students who carry heavier loads (e.g., 15 or 18 hours) would spend correspondingly more time studying, making their time commitment more like that of doctors, lawyers, executives, entrepreneurs, or college faculty.

Of course, this brings us back to the unfortunate disconnect that exists between the ideal represented by the rule of thumb and the reality of how much time most students are studying. The fact that students in the 1960s spent an average of about 24 hours per week studying outside class means that even then, the average was at the low end of the 2-to-3-hour rule of thumb. The fact that the average study time has now dropped to about 14 hours means that the average student today is putting in barely half as much study time as the rule of thumb would indicate to be necessary for success in learning college-level material. Again, if we accept that you must study to learn, then we are forced to conclude that today's students are not learning what we would like them to learn in college. That is why this first general teaching suggestion is so important: Our teaching success depends on finding a way to get our students to put in sufficient study time.

NOTE: STUDENTS DO NOT KNOW THE RULE OF THUMB Although the 2-to-3-hour rule of thumb is fairly well known among college faculty, I've informally polled thousands of freshmen and have found that very, very few have ever heard of it or been told about it. Moreover, their prior experience would lead them to conclude that far less studying is required. For example, they almost certainly did not put in that much study time outside class in high school, and for non-science majors, I've generally found that they report getting good grades in most of their classes without putting in anywhere near the rule of thumb amount of study. In other words, *there is no a priori reason why students should have any idea that you will expect them to study 2 to 3 hours outside class for each hour in class*. Which means you will need to tell them (more on that below).

NOTE: FOR SCIENCE, THE MAIN ISSUE IS IN NONMAJOR COURSES It's also worth reiterating the fact that for college science, the disconnect between expectations and reality applies primarily to nonmajor intro-ductory courses. As noted earlier, the data indicate that students in STEM fields (science, technology, engineering, and math) are study-ing more than students in other majors, and those of you teaching upper-division courses in these fields probably have your students working quite hard. Moreover, if you look at long-term teaching success, the fact that the United States is still a clear global leader in science and engineering (and that students from all over the world come here to study in those disciplines) tells us that our college edu-cation for science majors *is* succeeding. In contrast, the continued low level of basic scientific literacy among the general public indicates that we are not yet succeeding as well as we would like at educating our students in nonmajor introductory science courses.

▶ **K–12 Education**: Unlike the case for college, there is no general consen-sus on the appropriate amount of homework for K–12 students. Never-theless, a visit to almost any elementary school classroom will demon-strate an important point about time on task: Even during class, students spend most of their time working independently (or in small groups). Again, this is as it should be; it would clearly be counterproductive for an elementary teacher to spend the day lecturing, so teachers spend most of their time allowing their students to work while they provide guid-ance as needed. In other words, most of the students' time on task occurs through independent work rather than during any sort of lecture or whiteboard time.

NOTE: THE HOMEWORK DEBATE With regard to the homework debate, my own view is that we should ensure at least some daily reading and math drill outside of class even as early as first grade. Homework, by which I mean both actual work outside school and work completed during in-school study time (including time spent working independently in class), should then gradually ramp up so that by the end of high school, the combination of class time and homework is close to a college expectation. Be sure to recognize that because high school students spend more hours *in* class than college students, they need fewer outside hours to reach the same total time on task.

NOTE: HELPING STUDENTS WHO LACK HOME SUPPORT I'll also reiterate my earlier point about the practical reality that students from lower-income families or with less-educated parents have less opportunity for academic support at home. This again argues for providing more in-school study time for these students, so that they have the opportunity to complete the work that is expected of them.

Educating Students about Time-on-Task Expectations: If we want students to put in as much time on task as we think necessary for their success, then we need to be sure they are aware of our expectations. As I've noted, college students by and large are unfamiliar with the rule of thumb, and K–12 students also often are unsure of what their teachers expect. Therefore, at least one key to successfully getting your students to study lies in making your expectations clear.

▸ **College Education**: I have found that you can often get college students to work much harder simply by telling them up front about the rule of thumb and your general workload expectations. For example, I provide students with a handout on how to succeed in college classes (the complete version is in Appendix 1) that discusses how to study and includes Table 1 below.

Table 1. College Study Time

If Your Course Is:	Time for Reading the Assigned Text (per week)	Time for Homework Assignments (per week)	Time for Review and Test Preparation (average per week)	Total Study Time (per week)
3 credits	2 to 4 hours	2 to 3 hours	2 hours	6 to 9 hours
4 credits	3 to 5 hours	2 to 4 hours	3 hours	8 to 12 hours
5 credits	3 to 5 hours	3 to 6 hours	4 hours	10 to 15 hours

If you discuss this table and its implications on the first day of class, you may preempt many of the problems that might otherwise arise from insufficient study time. For example, if a student comes to you in office hours expressing difficulty in understanding the course material, you can start by asking the student how much he or she is studying. If it is less than the expected study time, then the student's problem is likely that he or she is not studying enough. If it is the expected time or more than the expected time, and if you are unable to answer the student's questions quickly and easily, then it is likely that the student is studying inefficiently. In that case, you might point the student to resources designed to improve study skills; many colleges have counseling or special programs designed to help students improve their study skills, and these days you can also find a variety of online videos designed to do the same. (A student might struggle is if he or she is missing some expected prerequisite background, in which case you'd need to discuss whether and how the student can make that up.)

NOTE: STUDENTS FOR WHOM THE RULE OF THUMB CANNOT FIT THE ACTUAL NUMBER OF HOURS IN A WEEK When you present the rule of thumb, you will undoubtedly be confronted by at least some students for whom personal circumstances may make this expectation unrealistic. For example, a full-time (12-credit-hour) student with a job and a family may simply not have enough hours in a week to put in the 24 to 36 hours of study suggested by the rule of thumb. While I'm very sympathetic to such students, I believe there is only one fair response to them: Help them realize that they have taken on too much at one time. In doing so, they have set themselves up for failure, and the best help you can offer is to be willing to discuss ways in which they might adjust their schedules to increase their odds of success. In some cases, for example, you might recommend reducing course load and taking longer to graduate; in other cases, you might recommend that a student consider taking out loans rather than spending so much time at a job. Just remember that in all cases, the key point is that you need effort and study to learn. College is expensive in both time and money, and if students truly want to get the value they deserve, then they need to find a way to put in the necessary study time.

NOTE: POLICY CHANGES TO ALLOW STUDENTS MORE TIME TO GRADUATE Today, there are far more students than in the past for whom family or other obligations may make a 4-year college path unrealistic, at least if we expect study at the level of the rule of thumb. Unfortunately, current college policies don't offer much help to such students, in part because most colleges charge tuition and fees per term. I therefore hope that college administrators will do some "outside the box" thinking to help these students find an appropriate path to a degree. For example, perhaps colleges might offer a total price for a degree if finished within some period (say, 7 or 8 years), paid in prorated amounts as coursework progresses. I do not know that this approach would work, but we need to find some alternatives for students who do not fit the traditional model of a recent high school graduate with no obligations besides study.

NOTE: IT'S OK TO TAKE LONGER Any suggestion that a student might consider taking longer to graduate is usually met negatively, at least at first. I believe there are two reasons for this. First, our culture has long focused on four years as the appropriate time to a degree, so any suggestion of taking longer may lead a student to feel in some way inadequate to meet the "normal" expectation. Second, an extra year or two or three tends to sound like a lot to students in their teens or twenties. It won't always work, but in these cases I've found that it helps to point out to students that in the long run, getting a degree that indicates real learning will be far more important than a couple of years right now. After all, when you're 50, you're likely to care far more about the kinds of jobs that your college education enabled you to get than you will about whether you graduated at 22 or 25.

NOTE: STUDENTS WHO COMPLAIN ABOUT THE RULE OF THUMB A related issue arises when your students realize that while *you* may be expecting them to follow the rule of thumb, most of their other teachers probably do not. Will they therefore think you are some kind of ogre? In some cases they probably will, but I've also found that students by and large are able to understand the expense of college (in both time and money) and recognize that it is only worthwhile if they actually learn something. As anecdotal evidence, I'll offer results that I've gotten in the past on end-of-course evaluations. My evaluations have included fill-in-the-bubble items for amount of study time and whether the study time was too much, too little, or just right. The majority of my students checked that they did indeed study the expected 6 to 9 hours per week outside my 3-credit class and that it was "just right." Yet, when I asked students to add comments about the workload, many of the very same students who checked that it was "just right" also wrote comments along the lines of "It was more than I studied for all my other classes combined." The lesson, I believe, is that students will think your workload is reasonable as long as they feel they've learned something of value (and as long as they knew from the start that you would expect this much work).

▶ **K–12 Education**: In terms of helping students understand the time on task that you expect from them, the only real difference between college and K–12 education is that for the latter, it's equally important to be sure that *parents* understand what you expect. These days, most teachers are pretty good about sending home information sheets or e-mails that explain the expectations for homework and study, and many districts have web sites where parents can check the progress of their children. Just keep in mind that some parents are difficult to reach, may ignore handouts, may not have a computer, may not know how to access a school web site, or may not speak English. If you want all of your students to put in the study time you expect, you'll need to find some way to reach all of their parents.

Implications of Time on Task: The expectations for study time that we've discussed lead to an important observation: *The time during which you have some form of direct communication with your students should be no more than a relatively small fraction of their total time on task for your course.* For college students, the rule of thumb tells us that time in class should represent no more than 1/4 to 1/3 of a student's total time on task for a course. K–12 students will have more time in class, but as we've discussed, most of this time will still be spent on independent work (with the teacher providing guidance rather than direct instruction).

The implication should be clear: While you should do everything you can to make good use of your class or direct-contact time, the even more important component of your teaching success will be in how well you manage students' independent study time — an idea that will bring us to my next general suggestion for teaching.

NOTE: ON "TEACHING TO THE TEST" The time-on-task issues raise a very important point about what is sometimes called "teaching to the test." The point is that while this type of teaching is sometimes necessary — after all, part of your job as a teacher is to make sure your students pass their tests — it is by no means sufficient. The problem is that tests (espe-

Five General Suggestions

cially multiple choice) tend to cover only the most easily measurable aspects of learning, which means they are heavy on basic facts and skills, and much lighter on conceptual understanding. Indeed, I'd argue that many of the most subtle levels of conceptual understanding are not truly testable.

As a somewhat extreme example, consider the physics of the atom, more generally known as quantum mechanics. Given that even Nobel Prize winners argue about whether anyone truly "understands" quantum mechanics, how could you ever test whether a student has developed a deep conceptual understanding of the subject versus having simply become good at doing the necessary calculations? In the end, I don't think there's any getting away from the fact that the more students study, the deeper the understanding that they'll build — whether you can test it or not. So teach to the test if you must, but don't stop there, or else you will be depriving your students of the opportunity to truly learn your subject matter.

NOTE: THE VALUE AND LIMITATIONS OF EDUCATIONAL RESEARCH A related point concerns educational research, which also by necessity tends to focus on the more easily measurable parts of learning. This limitation does not in any way reduce the value of educational research, which has turned up numerous important results that can point the way to improvements in teaching for today's mass-production settings. But even the best research can backfire when people forget its limitations. For example, at the college level, a great deal of educational research has focused on methods of making classrooms more dynamic and interactive, and these methods can significantly enhance student learning when implemented well. The problem I've sometimes seen is that faculty become so impressed with the improvements they are able to make *during* class that they forget the fact that class time should represent only a small fraction of total student time on task. In those cases, faculty may cut back on outside assignments, so that despite the success during class, students end up putting in so little outside study time that their total learning still falls far below the rule-of-thumb college expectation. The same idea also applies in K–12 settings, in which teachers running dynamic classrooms still need to assign appropriate amounts of independent or outside study.

NOTE: THE VALUE AND LIMITATIONS OF "FLIPPED CLASSROOMS" Continuing with a similar theme, it's worth saying a few words about "flipped classrooms," in which students are expected to learn new content at home (often by reading a textbook or watching video lectures, sometimes with online quizzing to confirm their understanding) *before* they come to class, so that they can then spend class time doing work that in the past would have been assigned as homework. This model can be extraordinarily successful, but only if you recognize its limitations.

The great benefit of the "flipped" model is that using class time for delivery of new content is demonstrably inefficient for student learning, especially when done in traditional "lecture mode." Therefore, having students attempt to learn the new content on their own allows class time to be used efficiently to fill in gaps in understanding and to offer personalized guidance to individual students. The limitation is simply the amount of class time available; for example, if college students spend an hour watching a video lecture and another hour doing "homework" in class, that's only two total hours of study time *including* the class time, far less than the rule of thumb of 2 to 3 hours *plus* the class time. My personal advice: I think "flipped classrooms" are a great idea — indeed, many great teachers have long done the equivalent by expecting students to come to class prepared to participate — but be sure you still assign enough total work to get the full time on task that we should be expecting of students.

General Teaching Suggestion 2

Provide structure and assignments that will help your students study *sufficiently* and *efficiently*.

Although success depends on study, not all study time is equal. Students who put in a lot of time may still not learn much if they use that time poorly. Therefore, a major part of your job as a teacher is to organize your course in ways that encourage your students to put in *sufficient* time to learn the course material while also helping to ensure that they make *efficient* use of that time.[3]

---

[3] A brief semantic note: Some faculty have asked if it would be better to say that students should make "effective" rather than "efficient" use of study time. Each word has its advantages, and I've left "efficient" in part because dictionaries and thesauruses generally list the two words as synonyms. However, it should not affect the rest of the discussion if you prefer to think in terms of effectiveness rather than efficiency.

Broadly speaking, you have two major opportunities for promoting this sufficiency and efficiency: (1) during class time in which you have direct contact with students; and (2) through the assignments you give to students. Let's briefly look at ways that you can make the most of these opportunities.

Class/Direct-Contact Time: As we've discussed, direct-contact class time should represent only a relatively small fraction of your students' total time on task. For this reason, I believe the most important use of this time is not in covering any particular parts of your curriculum, but rather in providing students with the motivation and guidance they need to make good use of the rest of their time on task.

What is the best way to provide motivation and guidance during class time? Everyone has an opinion, and educational research tells us that more interactive methods tend to give better results, but the bottom line is this: *If you get your students to study (sufficiently and efficiently), then your methods are successful*; if your students don't study, then you should be seeking to revise your methods.

Of course, some methods of teaching are more likely than others to provide that motivation for study, and I believe the general guideline is the following: *The key to motivating students is to get them to pay attention.* This fact explains why traditional "lecture mode" (in which an instructor talks while standing at a whiteboard or doing PowerPoint projections) is usually one of the least effective methods of motivating students: Unless you are a particularly dynamic lecturer, this mode makes it too easy for students to allow their attention to drift while you speak. With that in mind, here are a few suggestions for holding students' attention during class time; as usual, they are aimed primarily at science teachers but may be adapted to other subject areas:

- *Share your enthusiasm.* If you want students to care about the subject matter you are covering in class, you need to show them that *you* care about it. This should not be hard to do in principle, since you presumably became a science teacher because of your passion for science. Nevertheless, there's at least some truth to the stereotype of scientists as shy and introverted, and if you fall into that category, then you need to make an extra effort to step out and share your own enthusiasm with your students. Note that humor can be useful, because it can help relax both you and your students; you may also want to bring in cartoons relevant to the topic you are covering. (On the latter point, it's worth spending a little time browsing collections of cartoons that relate to science. Classic sources include The Far Side, Calvin and Hobbes, Dilbert, Foxtrot, and the work of Sidney Harris [sciencecartoonsplus.com]; I also like many of the cartoons by Randall Munroe at xkcd.com.)

- *Use demonstrations, props, and experiments.* We've already briefly discussed the value of visualizations, and some of the best types of visualization result from the use of demonstrations, props, and experiments. These are useful not only in explaining scientific concepts, but also in making your classes more memorable to students. Think back to your own college science days, and you almost undoubtedly will recall amazing demonstrations much more than amazing lectures. Even if a particular demonstration or prop seems extremely simplistic, it's likely to be better than nothing at all. And if you can turn your demonstration into something students can experiment with themselves, it's likely to go over even better.

  NOTE: DISCREPANT EVENTS Educators define "discrepant events" as events that disagree with what students expect to see. These are very common in science; to take a simple example, most students guess wrong about what will happen when you swing a ball around on a string and then let go of it. Although a discrepant event demonstration may take only a few minutes and can be done with household or common classroom materials, the lesson may stick with students for a lifetime. A YouTube search on "discrepant events" will lead you to many easy-to-replicate demonstrations.

  NOTE: ROLE PLAYING Another type of "demonstration" that has been used successfully by many great teachers is to have your students role play. For example, you can have your students play roles in physical systems to demonstrate such things as planetary motion (one student is the Sun, others are planets) or interactions in a cell. Similarly, you might engage students in a famous debate from history, such as whether Earth is the center of the universe or a planet going around the Sun; you might make it even more fun by coming to class dressed as Galileo. (In biology or Earth science, if you aren't intimidated by the public debate, come as Darwin and have students debate the meaning of the evidence you present for evolution.) These types of role play can be particularly successful with middle and high school students, though they can work at any age.

- *Move when you talk.* If you just stand there, you look bored. Be animated as you explain important concepts. Even when you don't have a demonstration or prop, you can often use movement to aid your explanations; as a simple example, if you're talking about phases of the Moon and don't have Styrofoam spheres handy, it's still useful to use one fist as Earth and the other as the Moon as you explain the Moon's orbit. You should also move around the classroom, so that you're not always looking at the same students; in many cases, the mere act of making direct eye contact can be enough to recapture a student's wandering attention.

- *Be Socratic.* There's a reason that the Socratic method of asking questions (sometimes referred to simply as the "questioning" technique) has been in use for thousands of years: because it works. When you ask a question, you force a student both to pay attention and to think (of course, you must be careful to pause long enough for students to think about the answer, but not so long that their attention will wander — an idea you'll sometimes hear expressed as "wait time"). The old law school method is to call out individual students essentially at random, under the assumption that this technique forces all the students to listen closely enough to be able to answer. Elementary school teachers are often taught a similar technique called "popsicle stick," in which each student's name is on a stick and the teacher draws a stick to call on someone to answer a question. An alternative approach is to ask the entire class a question; teachers have long done this by asking for a show of hands or for students to hold up index cards that indicate their responses. Today, it is common to use clickers, which offer at least three potential advantages: (1) Clickers ensure that every student records a response (or is recorded as a nonresponse). (2) Clickers provide data on the overall class response, which can lead you as the teacher to recognize misconceptions that you might otherwise have missed. (3) The fact that clickers are anonymous to fellow classmates prevents students from embarrassment when they make a wrong choice, and tends to encourage honesty in responses rather than attempts to copy neighbors.

  NOTE: CLICKERS AND ATTENDANCE There's a fourth advantage to clickers for large college classes: They provide a means of taking attendance. While there is room for debate, I personally believe that attendance should be required; after all, you can't motivate students who don't show up. For example, in my 3-times-a-week college classes, I generally told students that more than 3 unexcused absences would result in reducing their final grade by ⅓ of a grade point (e.g., from B to B−), with each pair of subsequent absences subtracting another third of a grade point. Of course, if you do this, you need to explain what constitutes an "excused" versus an "unexcused" absence. My policy was generally to be liberal with excused absences when students alerted me to them ahead of time, but to excuse after the fact only if they provided documentation of illness or some type of unexpected emergency.

- *Promote controlled interaction.* You're probably aware of many techniques that have been promoted for making classrooms more interactive, ranging from short breaks for students to discuss questions with each other to "flipped classrooms" in which the instructor acts primarily as a facilitator for individual or group activities. These methods can be very effective, because interactivity demands attention. They are therefore worth doing, though you should keep at least four cautions in mind:

   1. Students are inevitably at different levels, so you must take care to ensure that an interactive activity that is useful to one student isn't overly simplistic or overly complicated to others.

   2. In group work situations, some students are expert at getting others to do their work for them, so you must ensure that credit is based on actual effort within a group, not simply on being a member of a group that does well.

   3. Interactivity usually takes more time for a particular topic than, say, asking a clicker question, and you must therefore be careful not to overdo the interactives to the point of not having time to complete the key material for your course.

   4. Keeping control of a classroom in which students are talking and working together can be much more challenging than it is for a classroom in which students are sitting quietly in their chairs; therefore, if you're going to do interactives, you must be sure that you are able to maintain students' respect for your classroom authority.

   NOTE: USE COOPERATIVE LEARNING STRATEGIES In educational research, techniques for classroom interaction are generally known as "cooperative learning strategies." Many such strategies have been developed and validated by research; a few popular ones go by names such as "think-pair-share," "round table," and "three-minute review." When used successfully, these strategies force individual students to

Five General Suggestions

think carefully about what they are learning; that is, they take owner-ship of their learning. A quick web search will provide you with infor-mation on how to implement these and other cooperative learning strategies.

NOTE: MORE ON CLASSROOM CONTROL Following up on the fourth point above, some teachers have personalities that make it very difficult for them to keep control once a classroom begins to get active. This does not make them bad teachers; it just means they may be less effective than other teachers at implementing some types of interac-tivity. If you happen to fall into this category, your first line of defense should be to make sure you have studied cooperative-learning strat-egies so that you are implementing them as intended; you may also benefit from attending a workshop on the implementation of these strategies. And if that fails, don't despair; you can still be successful in the classroom through other strategies, with success measured by how well you motivate students to do their sufficient and efficient studying.

- *Don't expect to cover everything.* One issue that almost all science teach-ers at all levels face is that there simply isn't enough class time to cover all of the material that your students are expected to know by the end of your course. The message here should be that this is OK. Remember, your students will do most of their learning without you, so there's no reason why you need to cover everything in class. Just be sure that if you don't cover something in class, you still have assignments that will help students learn whatever it is that they need to learn.

- *Provide feedback.* Perhaps it goes without saying, but as you engage in all the above practices, be sure that you provide students with clear feedback about their work in class. After all, without feedback, students will be working in the dark, unaware of whether they are meeting your expectations. Although much of your feedback may be given to students outside class time (through marked-up assignments, or direct speaking or e-mails), good teachers also provide real-time feedback, and the best manage to individualize the feedback even in the classroom setting.

NOTE: APPLICATION TO ONLINE COURSES All of the above suggestions obviously apply to physical classrooms, as opposed to online courses. Nevertheless, the principle of motivating your students to study still applies if you are teaching an online course, though you may need to find alternative ways to do it.

NOTE: ON SELF-PACED LEARNING I've also assumed that your class involves directed learning as opposed to self-paced learning. (Directed learning can still be individualized so that different students progress at different paces; by "self-paced" I mean a situation in which students actually set their own pace, without a teacher's direct guidance.) I won't comment on how to motivate students in the self-paced environment for two reasons: First, self-paced courses by definition don't really have a "teacher," so it's unlikely that you'd be teaching one (though you might be "managing" one); second, and more important, my opinion is that with rare exceptions, self-paced courses are a very bad idea, because they make it too easy for students to procrastinate (and it's a rare human being who doesn't at least occasionally fall into the procrastination trap). Indeed, if self-paced learning actually worked for most people, then we wouldn't need schools or teachers, since students would find it cheaper to learn on their own. Also worth remembering: Learning on your own does not require expensive modern technology; it has long been possible to learn on your own by going to the library. Some highly motivated people have indeed learned that way in the past, but such people represent a small fraction of all students to whom we hope to deliver mass-produced education.

NOTE: ON MOOCS ("MASSIVE OPEN ONLINE COURSES") Despite the skepticism I express above about self-paced learning and learning without classrooms and teachers, there's a huge push under way to promote so-called MOOCs, in which a single outstanding professor may have tens to hundreds of thousands of students enrolled in a course. This idea is especially popular with administrators and politicians, who see it as a way to deliver more education for less money. There are at least two clear benefits to MOOCs: (1) They can help democratize education by providing it to people who otherwise could not afford it or live in places (especially in the developing world) where educational access is limited, and (2) Assuming that faculty are well-chosen and assignments developed with great care, then MOOCs can in essence deliver "best of the best" lectures and assignments to highly motivated students.

Nevertheless, for all but the most highly motivated students, it seems virtually inconceivable to me that they could succeed as well or learn as much in a MOOC as they could in an actual, in-person course with a teacher. So unless solid data someday prove me wrong, I'll continue to believe that MOOCs should be an option only for those who cannot get education some other way, and that *the best way to educate the majority of students is to have them attend classes with teachers.* (That said, there may still be value in the videos and assignments offered by MOOCs; I just think they are best used in conjunction with a physical class and an in-person teacher.)

Assignments: Given that your students will do most of their learning without direct input from you, how can you make sure that they spend enough time studying and that they use their study time efficiently? The answer is through assignments, which are in essence your way of trying to "force" students to do the studying necessary for success.

There are a variety of different types of assignments, but we can generally divide them into three major categories (which are essentially the same categories listed in Table 1 on p. 30):

1. *Reading.* This category primarily means assigned reading from a textbook or other required materials, though in today's world we should think of it somewhat more broadly as anything that involves absorbing material that has been recorded in any medium, whether print, electronic, or video. Therefore, I put such things as online research and videos that you ask students to watch into this "reading" category, and it may also include embedded interactives in digital media. Moreover, it's a good idea to encourage students to take notes in their own words as they read (or watch, etc.), and this note taking also counts as "reading time," since it is designed to help students understand and reflect on what they read.

2. *Homework/Independent Assignments.* This category means any kind of student work that could in principle be assessed or graded, whether it is traditional homework problems, drills, writing assignments, projects, or group activities. Note also that it does not necessarily have to be done outside of school; in many cases, at least some of this work can be done during class, or in special in-school study periods in K–12 education.

3. *Exam Preparation.* Although we usually don't think of exam preparation as something that we "assign" to students like reading or homework, the mere act of scheduling an exam means that students will need to study for it.

Because your goal is to make sure that your students study sufficiently and efficiently, the primary challenge of assignments lies in making sure they require the right amount of work, appropriately balanced among the three general categories, and making sure the work is high quality. Meeting this challenge is an art that you'll improve through practice, but I'll give a few suggestions that may help.

Reading: Reading is generally most valuable if students do it *before* you talk about something in class (which is one reason that "flipped classrooms" are becoming more popular). This is especially true at the high school and college levels, though it is a skill that younger children should be building as well. The difficulty, of course, is that there is no way for you to force students to read the assigned material, nor to monitor whether they are paying close attention to the reading versus letting it go in one eye and out the other. Nevertheless, there are some carrots and sticks you can use to encourage students to read well. For example, if you have a small (or "flipped") class, you may be able to provide classwork or hold class discussions in which students benefit from having done the reading and pay a price for not having done so (which might be a price in grades, or a behavioral price such as being sequestered in a side room until the student catches up on missed preparation work). For larger classes, you can use online quizzes to encourage reading (e.g., require your students to complete an online reading quiz prior to the class in which the material will be covered), or use an occasional pop quiz in class to check what they've learned from the reading.

Homework/Independent Assignments: First, let me re-emphasize a critical point: While good-quality homework is invaluable, poorly thought out "busywork" is just a waste of everyone's time. Again, the key words are *sufficient* and *efficient*; student study time should be both.

We've already discussed the amount of time that constitutes sufficient study at different levels, so let's focus here on the question of how to make sure that students can study efficiently. Part of that, of course, depends on their having built good study habits; if they haven't, it will be worth your time to help them with that (especially if you teach elementary or middle school, where your students may not have had prior opportunities to develop study skills), or to point them to other resources (e.g., counselors, special programs, online videos) that can help.

The second part of ensuring that study time is used efficiently falls on you as the teacher: You need to make sure that what you assign is valuable to student learning. Like much of teaching, determining the value of a particular assignment is more of an art than a science, but here are a few ideas that you may find useful:

Five General Suggestions

- *Activate the brain.* Suppose you read a science article in a journal. Which will help you absorb the concepts better: reading it twice, or reading it once and then going through it a second time and taking notes as you do so? Most people find the second strategy much more effective, and I believe that the reason has been explained by brain research: Writing appears to activate different areas of the brain than reading, which suggests that doing both helps build more neural connections. The same appears to be true of other types of learning activities, with each type activating different brain functions. Therefore, within the confines of what is reasonable for your course, you should strive to have assignments include a variety of tasks, such as writing, simple recall, critical thinking and reasoning, hands-on experiments, individual work, and group work.

- *Practice and drill (but don't kill).* Sometimes there are facts and methods that we just need our students to learn, and repeated practice can be a very effective way to learn them. To take an example that everyone is familiar with, kids simply can't learn their multiplication tables without spending a lot of time practicing them. That said, finding the right amount of practice and drill is an important art, so you should closely monitor students to make sure that you are giving them enough practice to become competent while not driving them insane with tedium.

  NOTE: THERE'S NO SUCH THING AS "DUMB MISTAKES" Imagine taking an algebra test. You understand all the concepts clearly, but somewhere along the way you make a few errors and end up with a lower score than you expected. It's tempting to think that you really do understand the test material and simply made "dumb mistakes," and that's what most of our students think when it happens to them. But there's no such thing as dumb mistakes; instead, there are mistakes that can be traced to insufficient practice. To take an analogy, imagine learning to play a favorite song on your guitar. You know exactly what the song is supposed to sound like (analogous to understanding the concept), but you'll make plenty of mistakes the first few (or few dozen) times you play it. On the guitar — or on any instrument, or in dance, or in sports — we know that the reason for these mistakes is that it takes practice to learn something new; hence the old idiom "Practice makes perfect." You can use this fact to explain the importance of practice and drill to your students. After all, they know that they need practice in music, dance, and sports, so why should they expect it to be any different in academics?

NOTE: GAMES CAN HELP For K–12 education, there are now thousands of apps and games that can support kids by making practice and drill more fun in math, science, and much more. Many are free, so it's definitely worth exploring options that can take some of the tedium out of important drill and practice time.

- *Return again and again.* If you want your students to retain something, then you should come back to it over and over again. For complex concepts, you can add a little more detail or depth with each return. This idea has traditionally been called "spiral learning," because a rising (three-dimensional) spiral returns to the same planar position over and over but at a higher level each time. (More recently, educational researchers have taken to calling it "spaced repetition," because you space out the times at which you return to the same topic.) The idea is relatively easy to implement both in class and in assignments, as it simply means that you expect students to be able to deal with the same kinds of questions that you give them early in the course when it gets later in the course, perhaps with some added depth. Worth noting: In many ways this idea shapes the entire science curriculum from preschool through graduate school, because much of science education involves returning to the same topics year after year, but with greater depth as students become more sophisticated in their thinking abilities.

- *Mix it up.* You've probably seen the kinds of math homework assignments that begin with something like "The following problems require use of the quadratic formula." This may be fine when you are first teaching students to use the formula, but if you're trying to build problem-solving skills, then it's counterproductive to tell the students exactly what they'll need to do to solve the problem. To generalize, the idea is that *except* when you are deliberately focusing on drill (as above), you should mix up the types of problems that you give so that students will have to think about the problem rather than applying some rote process. (This strategy also has a new name in educational research; it's called "interleaving.")

  NOTE: PROBLEM-SOLVING STRATEGIES Given that one of the major goals of education is for students to develop problem-solving skills, you may want to spend a little time discussing problem-solving strategies. The classic work in this area, which is still immensely valuable, is George Polya's book *How to Solve It*. For a somewhat simplified and easier-to-remember version of Polya's approach, I suggest "Under-stand-Solve-Explain" (which has the simple acronym U-S-E). With this approach, the first step is to be sure you understand the problem you are trying to solve; for example, what will your final solution look like, and what information do you need in order to proceed? The second step is to carry out the work needed to come up with a solution, such as any mathematical calculations required. The third and final step is to explain your solution, which you should do in a way that both confirms that your solution makes sense and is clear enough for others (including the teacher who assigned the problem) to follow so that they will understand what you've learned.

My final comment on homework concerns grading. Once you have developed your homework or independent assignments, your next big challenge is likely to be grading them. Indeed, unless you have a very small class, you're likely to find that assigning enough homework will produce more of a grading burden than you can realistically handle. For these cases, you'll need to come up with some way of dealing with the grading problem. Some of you may be fortunate enough to have a budget available to hire grading help. If you don't have that, then an excellent alternative is to use some of today's online systems that do automatic grading, fed back to your course gradebook. In fact, although these systems do not have the flexibility of written homework, the good ones have the advantage of providing students with instantaneous feedback, which has benefits that are difficult to get in other ways. If you don't have online systems, or for homework that isn't suited to auto grading (essay answers, group work, etc.), then you may wish to fall back on old strategies such as grading only selected problems from assignments or having students grade their own or each other's work. Indeed, this can even be advantageous, especially in K–12 education, where giving students the ability to correct and improve their own work helps them take ownership of their learning.

NOTE: ON GRADING SELECTED PROBLEMS If you choose to grade only selected problems, you're likely to have some students complaining about fairness (e.g., "I did all the others correctly but you only graded the one that I missed!"). Although it does not always work, I've found that the best response is to ask students if your assignments are helping them learn (for which the answer will probably be yes if you're giving high-quality assignments) and then asking if they'd still do the assignments if you made them optional. Most students will admit that they're more likely to do work that is required, and most also understand that you're human and can do only so much grading. They may still not like the selective grading, but they'll understand why it is necessary. I've also had some success with selective grading by basing part of the total grade on a broad overview of the student's work. For example, on a 10-point homework assignment, I might assign 4 points to each of two problems that I grade in depth, while full credit on the final 2 points requires that the entire assignment be complete and at least appear to show careful work.

NOTE: PROMPT FEEDBACK AND RECORD KEEPING Though it might seem obvious, remember that prompt feedback is very important to student learning; the longer you delay delivering feedback to students, the less of an impact your comments will have, because students will have lost the train of thought that led to the work they turned in. Along the same lines, careful record keeping is also critical, because students count on you to keep track of their performance. Although software now makes record keeping much easier than it was in the past, you still need to be diligent to be sure everything is recorded clearly. And don't forget to have backups — both electronic and printed — in case computers crash or files become corrupted.

Exam Preparation: The mere term "testing" tends to carry a lot of negative connotations, but while many of those are well deserved, testing can also be an outstanding tool for learning. The reason is simple: After students have done all the reading, all the homework, and all the in-class activities and discussions, they still need to take time to step back to reflect on and consolidate everything they've done. While you can sometimes help them with this consolidation by assigning projects or papers, testing is often the most practical way to encourage it. Education researchers refer to this idea as "retrieval practice": By forcing students to retrieve knowledge for the test, we reinforce that knowledge.

The fact that testing is a learning tool leads me to at least five specific suggestions:

1. *Tests should help students learn.* While any test will mean students need to study, you should strive to design your tests to serve the goal of helping students learn. That is, try to write questions that make students really think about what they are doing. For example, if you are writing a multiple-choice question, make sure the incorrect choices

(sometimes called the "distractors") are reasonable enough to make students think carefully. For a short-answer or problem-solving question, you should expect students to explain their work clearly enough not only to demonstrate that they know the answer, but also so they could go back and study from their own answer in the future. (Of course, be sure that you communicate your expectations clearly to students.)

> **NOTE: PROS AND CONS OF MULTIPLE CHOICE** Some of you may be wondering about multiple choice (or other objective question types) versus questions that require writing. My own belief is that both options have their advantages; in particular, while the latter is probably a better test of learning on any particular question, the former is faster and therefore allows you to test over a wider range of topics. You should decide how to balance the question types on your tests based on your own course goals, as well as on practical considerations such as how long it will take to grade the tests. In some cases, you may also want to consider the option of "combination" multiple-choice questions, in which students must not only select an answer but also include a brief written explanation of why they think their answer is correct.

2. *Tests should reflect assignments.* Because a major goal of testing is to encourage students to study the other work you've assigned, I believe it is important to write tests that reward those students who've done the work diligently. One way to do this is by making sure that your test closely follows other assigned work; I recommend repeating at least some questions they've seen on homework or other quizzes almost verbatim, which effectively rewards those who have studied the most.

> **NOTE: WHAT TO TEST IN INTRODUCTORY COURSES** A related point is especially important to those of you teaching nonmajor college courses: Be careful about asking questions designed to see if students can "take it to the next level" on the exam. While such questions can check deep understanding, they also tend to reward students who happen to come to your class with prior knowledge, rather than students who have learned a lot in your class. For a nonmajor class, I think that if students learn the material you've been teaching them, then they deserve to score well on the exam.

3. *Tests should be cumulative.* Although there's often debate over whether tests should be cumulative or only on the material covered most recently in class, I would argue that they should always be cumulative. After all, if you don't expect students to remember something even from one test to the next, what was the value in asking them to learn it in the first place? That said, there are certainly cases where it makes sense to have a short quiz that assesses only a particular unit, as long as students aren't given the impression that it's OK to forget what has come before.

4. *Frequency of tests should be "just right."* Without overdoing it, you should have enough tests to make sure that you are encouraging students to consolidate their learning on a semiregular basis. If your tests come too far apart, then you're asking students to do more consolidation at one time than is likely to be realistic. The difficult part, of course, is deciding what is "just right." The answer will vary with grade level, subject material, and the diligence of your students; I suggest discussing with colleagues what works best for a particular situation.

5. *Get students to review their tests.* Students are tempted to forget about a test once it is passed. However, if you've written a good test, then it will be to their benefit to go back and study it, especially the questions that they've missed. There are several ways in which you can encourage this type of review. One of the most common strategies, particularly in K–12 education where there is more class time available, is to spend time going over the test in the next class period. Another strategy is to repeat questions from prior exams on the next exam, so that students will know it's worthwhile to review.

> **NOTE: "EXAM REBATES"** A strategy that I've used successfully is what I call "exam rebates": I allow students to improve their grade by offering an opportunity to earn a "rebate" of up to *half* the points they lost on the original test. To earn the rebate, they must turn in a written summary in which, for each question that they missed, they explain both the correct answer and what was wrong with their original answer. When students do a good job of this, it really helps them correct their misunderstandings and do better for the rest of the course. The only downside to the exam rebates is that they can be grading intensive; to keep the grading load reasonable, you may wish to base the rebate on only a spot check of the complete written summary.

Five General Suggestions

Grading: All the above raises the question of how to weight grading. There's no single formula, because too many factors can affect the specifics. For example, while it might in principle be reasonable to assign 50% of the grade to homework, you probably won't want to do so if you have online assignments for which some students may have access to much more personal help than other students (which in some cases reaches the level of cheating if the student gets too much help from someone else). On the other hand, in some advanced science courses the homework may be so involved that you'll want to make it much more than 50% of the grade. Similarly, while reading is an important component of study, you may not be able to assign any portion of the grade to it unless you have online reading quizzes for students to do. The bottom line is the same as the one we arrived at earlier: If your system is working at getting students to study sufficiently and efficiently, then stick with it; if it isn't, then modify it.

NOTE: THE PROBLEM OF GRADE INFLATION The issue of grading naturally brings up the issue of grade inflation. This is a clear problem in our educational system, and not one that is easy to deal with. All I'll say here is that while we often lament the way grade inflation makes it difficult for teachers and administrators to differentiate student achievement, the real victims of it are our students. If we make it too easy to get the A, then students will not have to study as much and therefore won't learn as much; grade inflation also effectively punishes the best students, because they may end up with the same grade as others who worked and learned much less. So when you are deciding how to assign your grades, it may help to think about a piece of advice that I was once given by University of Colorado anthropology professor Jack Kelso, who ran an honors program for which I was teaching: "The only thing that you can do to a student that is worse than giving them a bad grade is giving them a grade that is higher than the one they deserve."

General Teaching Suggestion 3

Teach for the long term by focusing on three linked goals for science teaching: *education*, *perspective*, and *inspiration*.

It should go without saying that the major goal of teaching should always be the *long-term* success of our students. We want our students to be successful in their lives, in their careers, and in helping all of us win the "race between education and catastrophe" (from the H. G. Wells quote at the beginning of this book). We want the time during which students are enrolled in our courses to contribute to that success.

The difficulty, of course, is that teaching for the long term is easier said than done. As we discussed earlier, your assignments and tests can generally measure only short-term learning, since the students will be long gone from your classes by the time we can assess their long-term success. This fact makes it easy to lose the long-term focus, especially since students will push you to focus on "what's on the test." Therefore, my third general suggestion is to make an extra effort to keep your long-term focus despite the pressures to focus on the short term. In my own work, whether teaching, writing, or speaking, I find it helpful to think of long-term success in terms of three closely related goals:

- **Education**. Carefully consider the educational-content goals that will best support your students' long-term success. These will vary with grade level and course. In college, for example, the most important educational goals in a course for science majors will be to provide students with the prerequisite skills needed to move on to the next level, while the primary educational goal in courses for nonmajors will be a more general understanding and appreciation of science. K–12 educational goals will include both a general understanding/appreciation of science and preparation for their future classes.

- **Perspective**. As a science teacher, you undoubtedly believe that science is important to everyone's long-term success. Unfortunately, the statistics on science literacy show that a large segment of the public does not appreciate this importance, which means it will not be appreciated by many of your students (or their parents). Therefore, a second key goal of science education should be to show how science provides perspective on ourselves and on our planet; after all, it's hard to argue with the importance of perspective. The idea is embodied in a famous quote from T. S. Eliot; note that although you're most likely to hear this quote from astronomers, it is applicable to all the sciences, since all of science (indeed, all of education) is exploration on some level:

> We shall not cease from exploration
> And the end of all our exploring
> Will be to arrive where we started
> And know the place for the first time.
> —T. S. Eliot (from his poem *Little Gidding*)

You can in principle tie almost any particular piece of educational content to how it affects our perspective. If you put this principle into practice, it will not only make your class more interesting and worthwhile to your students, but it will also help you keep your own sense of awe, because it's likely to be perspective that got you excited about science in the first place.

- **Inspiration.** Think of a subject that you *don't* love; whatever it is, it's very likely that you can trace your lack of enthusiasm for it to some past teacher who made it seem dull. Now, think about your own love of science; you almost certainly acquired this love because you were inspired somewhere along the way, whether by a teacher, by a parent, or by some event you heard about through the media. (In my own case, for example, I can trace a large part of my inspiration to the Apollo missions that occurred in my youth.) The point is one we've already discussed: If you really want your students to succeed, you need to inspire them. Note that inspiration can occur on many levels, from the inspiration to learn this week's class material to the inspiration that turns science into a lifelong passion. But I hope everyone will seek to inspire students on at least this one particular level: Use science to inspire your students to dream of how they can personally contribute to helping all of us make a better world.

NOTE: THE UNFORTUNATE DECLINE OF FIELD TRIPS Do you remember the field trips you took in elementary, middle, or high school? Chances are that at least some of them were inspirational and still bring up fond memories. Sadly, field trips have been greatly de-emphasized in much of K–12 education, due to a combination of budget limitations and the additional time devoted to things like standardized tests. I don't have any great ideas on how to reverse this trend, but it should be clear that field trips can contribute greatly to the inspiration part of the "education, perspective, and inspiration" message. This is especially true for students who come from low-income or blue-collar families, because a field trip to a facility or business engaged in scientific or technological work may be the first time they see both the practical and the financial rewards of studying math and science. I hope that as a nation, we'll find some way to ensure high-quality field trips at least once a year throughout K–12 education.

Monetary Inspiration: As an idealist, I'd like to think that all our students will be inspired by the thought of making a better world. But realistically, at least some students respond more to money — especially in middle school and higher grades — so we might as well have something to hook them, too. Fortunately, this is very easy to do in education in general, and especially in science.

For education in general, here's a simple fact: Based on the latest available data (as of 2014), the median annual salary for college graduates (bachelor's degree) is approximately $28,000 higher than the median for those with only a high school diploma. Over a 40-year working career (say, ages 25 to 65), that translates to more than $1.1 million in additional earnings. In other words, while it's in vogue to complain about the high cost of college, on a median basis it is still about the best investment that a person can ever make. Moreover, while there is justified concern about unemployment among recent college graduates, the unemployment rate for those with college degrees is less than about half that of those without them. No matter how you look at it, education pays.

Now, remember that the values I've just given you are median values. The vast majority of the values at the high end come from STEM (science, technology, engineering, and mathematics) professions, and students who have learned more tend to do better than those who have learned less. In other words, if it will help inspire your students, here are three simple facts that you can give them:

- On average (median), doing well enough in school so that you end up graduating from a 4-year college will earn you more than $1 million "extra" over your lifetime, making a college education the monetary equivalent of winning the lottery.

- Data show that the vast majority of the careers with the *highest* median earnings are in areas that require substantial coursework or majors in science, technology, engineering, or mathematics. Working in one of these fields can easily increase your lifetime earnings by double, triple, or some higher multiple of the $1 million average.

- Furthermore, those who end up with the very highest earnings are usually those who learned the most in school. A small part of this can be attributed to the fact that many businesses look at grades when hiring, but the far more important aspect is that those who make the effort and put in the study time needed to succeed in school are far more prepared to give the same effort to their careers, and in the professional world that effort generally translates to more promotions and higher earnings. A simple example that applies to one of the most popular career choices: A nurse who is very strong in anatomy and physiology will likely be a better nurse than one who just got by in those courses, and is therefore more likely to be the one to receive promotions and salary boosts.

Elementary School Inspiration and Attitudes toward Science: All teachers at all levels should try to inspire students to gain appreciation of and motivation for science, but this is especially important for elementary teachers, because student attitudes begin to develop at young ages. Many elementary teachers are very good at helping students develop positive attitudes toward science, but there are also far too many cases in which elementary teachers have done just the opposite. The key factor seems to be the teacher's own attitude toward science: If *you* love science, so will your students, but if you fear it or have other negative attitudes toward it, you will find your negativity being transmitted to your students like an infectious disease. So if you are a teacher who doesn't already love teaching science, the first thing you need to do is to spend enough time studying science to overcome your own fears and negative attitudes. I'm sorry if this sounds harsh, but if you have negative attitudes toward science (or any other subject you are expected to teach) and aren't willing to make the effort to change those attitudes, then you don't belong in teaching.

NOTE: DON'T BE "BAD AT MATH" I should point out that a similar mindset is even more important for math, because far too many people consider it socially acceptable to say that they are "bad at math." Indeed, this is particularly problematic for elementary teachers, because surveys show them to be one of the most math-phobic groups in the United States (see McAnallen, Rachel R., Ph.D dissertation, "Examining Mathematics Anxiety in Elementary Classroom Teachers," U. Conn, 2010). So if you've ever been tempted to say "I'm bad at math" or "I'm not a math/science person," then it's time for an attitude transplant. (For those who may be interested, my book *Math for Life* is devoted in large part to the topic of attitudes toward mathematics.)

NOTE: HOW MUCH SCIENCE SHOULD ELEMENTARY TEACHERS KNOW? A related question for elementary teachers is how much science (and math) they should be expected to know. This can be debated to some extent, but my answer is that teachers at any level should know material well beyond what they are teaching their students. After all, students will be expected to learn more in future courses, and it's difficult to be an effective teacher if you aren't familiar with the material to which your students are heading. In high school, for example, we generally expect (or at least hope) that teachers will have majored in the subjects they are teaching, which means they'll have learned material that is at least 4 years ahead of the material they are teaching their students. Elementary teachers must teach a broad range of subjects, so we obviously can't expect them to have college major–level knowledge of all of them. Still, it seems reasonable to expect them to have at least the equivalent of a high school understanding of every subject they teach. Unfortunately, this is not always the case; for example, I've come across many teachers who are unable to help their own sons and daughters with even middle school homework in math and science. Again, my apologies for sounding harsh, but this seems completely unacceptable. Think about it this way: We'd never accept an elementary school teacher who can't read and write at an 8th-grade level, so why would we think it is OK for a teacher to be unable to do math or science at that same grade level?

Inspiring Girls and Young Women and Other Underrepresented Groups: It's well known that girls, young women, and members of several minority groups are underrepresented in science and other STEM fields, particularly those that involve physical science, computer science, and engineering. As a result, we need to make special efforts to inspire students from these groups. Many long articles and books have been written about how to accomplish this, so I won't say much about the details here. But I'll note just four issues that jumped out at me when I read those articles and books:[4]

1. *Confidence issues.* One key issue with underrepresented groups is self-confidence. Numerous studies (for example, Beilock, S. L., Rydell, R. J., and McConnell, A. R., *J. Exp. Psychology* 136, no. 2 (2007): 256–276) have documented what is known as "stereotype threat," in which girls and others subject to "bad at math/science" stereotypes actually perform more poorly when reminded of the stereotype and better when told the stereotype is false; one recent study even found that women perform better on math tests when they use fake names, which apparently made them less likely to fear that a negative stereotype would be confirmed for them as individuals (Zhang, S., Schmader, T., and Hall, W., *Self and Identity* 12, no. 4, May 2012).

---

[4] One summary article that I particularly recommend is "Why are there still so few women in science?" by Eileen Pollack, which appeared in the *New York Times Magazine* on October 6, 2013.

These and other studies seem to indicate that we should make special efforts to counter negative stereotypes for girls, women, and under-represented minorities. For example, we should work hard to help students build confidence in their abilities, and provide active encouragement to promising students about their potential future in science or other STEM fields. Some research even suggests that so-called achievement gaps can be eliminated when we succeed in getting students to overcome their confidence issues (for example, see Dweck, C., *Mindset*, Ballantine 2006).

> **NOTE: PERCEPTIONS OF STUDY AND EFFORT** Although I have not seen research on this particular point, anecdotal evidence suggests that there is a related issue that goes back to the importance of putting in plenty of study time and effort. If a girl or underrepresented minority student is not doing as well as we might hope in math or science, it is easy for both the student and the teacher to imagine that it is a result of inferior ability, much as the stereotypes might suggest. In fact, just as is the case with anyone else, the more likely problem is that the student simply is not putting in enough study and effort to succeed, probably because she or he doesn't realize how much study and effort is really required to learn math and science. I therefore believe it's especially crucial to remind students from underrepresented groups that math and science require hard work and effort, while at the same time emphasizing that if they put in this work, they can succeed just as well as anyone else.

2. *Hidden biases.* A recent study (Moss-Racusin, C., et al., *Proceedings of the National Academy of Sciences*, Sept. 17, 2012) found that when presented with hypothetical students with identical qualifications aside from their gender, academic scientists favored the male over the female, even when the scientists making the selection were women themselves. Clearly, we as a society still have deep-seated biases leading us to believe that women (and some minorities) aren't as good at science. It's not easy to eliminate this type of bias, but being conscious of its existence is an obvious first step.

3. *It's an American issue.* The general belief that women and minorities are less able to do science is more common in the United States than in many other countries and cultures. And just as you might expect from the paragraph about confidence issues above, those countries

and cultures that lack such biases are more likely to show more equal scientific achievement by groups that are underrepresented in the U.S.

4. *Role models.* Another related issue for women and underrepresented minorities is a lack of strong role models in science and other STEM fields. This makes it especially important to encourage those who have succeeded in science and STEM fields to be willing to speak out and encourage young people to follow their paths.

> **NOTE: BRING ROLE MODELS TO SCHOOL** For K–12 teachers, the last point above means you can have a big impact by contacting local scientists and engineers and recruiting them to come speak with and inspire your students. It is especially valuable if you can find role models who are female or who share ethnicity with some of your students. You'll have to give up a bit of class time to do this, but it will be well worth it. Indeed, while it won't happen every time, there are plenty of cases in which a single visit by a single inspiring professional has been the thing that turned some student's life around.

General Teaching Suggestion 4

Have high but realistic expectations, and spell them out clearly.

This one is probably self-explanatory, but to give you more detail I'll begin with one of my personal mantras about teaching: *We can't expect students to know what they've never been taught.* Sure, there are some exceptional students who will figure things out for themselves, but it's unreasonable to expect all students to do that. Therefore, if we want students to know something, and we suspect they've never learned it previously, then we need to teach it. The corollary to this idea is that we cannot expect students to read our minds about our expectations, either. That is, *we can't expect students to know what we expect, unless we tell them.*

Obvious as these ideas may seem, I've seen many cases in which they appear to have been forgotten, to the detriment of both teacher and students. On the knowledge side, I'll give you a simple example from college astronomy. In most college astronomy courses, professors take it for granted that students know that the Sun is a star. However, through informal surveys in my own courses, I have found that while almost all college students can recite the fact that "the Sun is a star," up to about a quarter of them do not truly grasp the fact that this means the Sun is the same type of object as the stars we see in the night sky. As you might imagine, students who lack this understanding can end up very confused if their instructor does not correct this deficiency before discussing the Sun and other stars. On the expectations side, recall our earlier discussions of how much we should expect students to study; as I noted, most students have never had to study in other subjects as much as we'll expect them to study in science, so unless you make that expectation clear, students may think they are incapable of understanding something when their real problem is simply that they haven't put in enough study time to absorb it.

Setting High but Realistic Expectations: If you are going to set high expectations, you're going to have to make some judgment calls about how high is still realistic. Like most everything in teaching, this call is more an art than a science. Nevertheless, I've found it helpful to focus on what I like to think of as two "guideposts" for teaching expectations:

- Guidepost 1: To ensure you are realistic, always assume that your audience members know *less* than you think they should.
- Guidepost 2: To ensure you reach high, always assume that your audience members are *more* intelligent than you think they are (or than they may think themselves to be).

We can use the "Sun is a star" example to illustrate these ideas. Most people teaching college astronomy assume their students should already know this type of basic fact. The first guidepost tells us that there's no harm in assuming that they don't; in this case, you'd begin your discussion of the topic of the Sun and other stars by saying something like "Remember that the Sun is a star, just like the stars we see in the night sky" (and perhaps remind them again of this fact from time to time). This clearly helps those students who may not have been aware of the fact, and it takes so little time and effort that it will not hurt the students for whom it is review; in fact, it may make them feel smart because they already knew it.

The second guidepost tells you not to think your students are dumb just because they didn't know some facts that you thought they should have known. In other words, once you've given them the needed review (which in this case is not much more than the single-sentence reminder), you should assume that they are an intelligent audience that is capable of learning higher-level concepts about the Sun and other stars.

NOTE: THE GUIDEPOSTS AND FEAR OF SCIENCE The latter point is particularly important in science, because it can be easy to mistakenly think that students are "dumb" when they are in fact only disengaged. Many students do poorly in science not because of a lack of intelligence, but rather because of a lack of comfort with or motivation for the subject matter — and sometimes an outright fear of it. In essence, the students create a self-fulfilling prophecy (sometimes called "learned helplessness") in which their discomfort leads them to be disengaged or disinterested, which in turn makes it more difficult for them to learn the material and increases their discomfort. The two guideposts can help you break this cycle, because the first guidepost will ensure that you don't leave them behind at the beginning, while the second ensures that you'll show them the kind of respect that can make them believe in their ability to learn your course material.

NOTE: THE GUIDEPOSTS AND NEGATIVE ATTITUDES TOWARD SCIENCE A corollary to the above note is that those students who enter your class knowing less than others are much more prone to feeling that they are "bad at science." The guideposts can help change such attitudes, because the first allows you to demonstrate that you aren't going to punish them for their lack of prior knowledge, while the second shows that you think they are smart and capable of learning. When students believe that *you* have confidence in their abilities, they are much more likely to gain the same confidence in themselves.

The two guideposts also tie back to the idea that we need to make sure we don't dumb down our courses (discussed earlier under One Key to Student Success). In essence, the guideposts show you how to meet your students at their level of understanding while still ensuring that you maintain high expectations. For example, I personally make use of them in my writing: The first guidepost reminds me to make sure that every topic in my books is introduced along with whatever prerequisite understanding is necessary for it, while the second reminds me not to skimp on the breadth and depth that I believe the subject matter should entail. Indeed, it is the fact that these two guideposts have proven so useful to me personally that leads me to hope that they will also be useful to you as you plan your teaching.

NOTE: USING THE GUIDEPOSTS WITH DIFFERENT AUDIENCES Following up on the idea that "brains are brains," the two guideposts can be helpful at almost any level. For example, if you are talking to children, you must

Five General Suggestions

answer their questions at a level they can understand (Guidepost 1) without being condescending or overly simplistic (Guidepost 2). At the other extreme, if you've ever been to a professional conference, you've undoubtedly heard research talks during which the speaker assumed you knew all kinds of things that you actually didn't know — in which case the talk was probably a waste of your time. The best talks are almost always the ones in which the speaker explains even the most basic ideas (Guidepost 1), while still teaching you something new and different (Guidepost 2).

Making Your Expectations Clear: If you want students to meet your high but realistic expectations, you need to make those expectations clear. This requires nothing more than clear communication. Starting with about middle school students, it's generally just a matter of having a clearly written syllabus so that students know exactly what to expect. For elementary school kids, you're more likely to tell them what you expect on a day-by-day basis rather than for a whole semester at a time, though you should be sure that parents know your plan for the entire year.

NOTE: BEHAVIORAL EXPECTATIONS Making your expectations clear applies both to content expectations (e.g., material to be covered, assignments that will be due) and behavioral expectations. The latter includes not only how much study time you expect outside class, but also how you expect students to behave in class. This is especially important for younger students, who may not yet have learned appropriate boundaries of respect for teachers. But it can also be true for college students. For example, these days it is not uncommon to have a few students who don't realize there's anything inappropriate about playing games on their cell phones during class. It may well be the case that they *should* know this, but since they don't, you have to tell them. Again, we can't expect students to know what they've never been taught, and it is at least conceivable that no one has ever called out a particular student for this type of behavior, in which case it's a lesson they've never been taught.

NOTE: SAMPLE SYLLABUS K–12 teachers are usually very good at making their expectations clear, perhaps in part because most school administrators expect it of them. College teachers, who may not get the same kind of administrative support, often have more difficulty in knowing how to lay out their expectations. For those of you who may feel that

you are in that position, Appendix 2 contains a sample college syllabus that you may feel free to borrow or adapt as needed for your own
classes.

Grading on Your Expectations: Again at the risk of stating the obvious:
It's critical that you base your grading on your expectations. After all, if you
tell the students they are expected to learn X and Y, but you grade on Z, it's
not only unfair but harmful to your reputation with future students. Perhaps a simple way to think of it is to remember that teaching is not a magic
show; our audience neither wants nor needs to be surprised. Rather, they
want to know exactly what they need to do to succeed in your class.

General Teaching Suggestion 5

Be human.

This last suggestion may seem a bit different in character from the others,
but it is very important. Teaching is arguably the most important profession
to our civilization's future, and you should take great pride in being the best
teacher you can possibly be and in striving to help every one of your students to succeed. But you are also a human being, which means there will
be days when you are not at your best, you'll make some mistakes, and you
won't be able to reach everyone. In other words, you cannot expect yourself
to be perfect.

This fact can even be turned to your advantage. It's *good* for your students to see that you are human, especially since the stereotype of scientists
and science teachers is often the opposite. You can also provide valuable lessons by modeling good ways of dealing with your human flaws. For example, if you had a bad day in class, then start with an apology the next time. If
you discover that you made a scientific error in an explanation, then at the
next class correct it without making excuses. And if something happens in
your life that is making it difficult for you to be at your best, don't be afraid
to share that fact with your students (though be careful not to provide "too
much information" about the details of your difficulties) — even very young
students can be remarkably understanding and even helpful.

Indeed, there are many ways that your humanity will affect both your
interactions with students and your own emotional well-being. Here are a
few more thoughts I've collected on this topic over the years, often from

Five General Suggestions

other teachers, and I'm sure you'll have other thoughts of your own to add to this list:

- *You can't reach everyone.* We all want a 100% success rate for our students, but it's simply not realistic. No matter how good a teacher you are and no matter how hard you work, you cannot reach everyone. For example, at the college level I'd estimate that at least 15% to 20% of your students in any given semester will be unreachable due to issues far beyond your control, such as illness, family issues, or boyfriend/girlfriend problems. In K–12 education, where students still live at home, the issues can be even more significant. For example, some students may be homeless, orphans, suffering abuse, or in the foster-care system. And, of course, a certain percentage of the population deals with mental illnesses (both diagnosed and undiagnosed), substance addictions, and other significant issues that will limit their ability to succeed in a classroom setting.

  NOTE: HELP YOUR STUDENTS GET HELP Keep in mind that while there may be nothing that *you* can do to address a particular student's situation, it's possible that others may be able to help — and that as a teacher, you may be seeing problems that might not be obvious to anyone else in that student's family or community. For that reason, you should always try to make sure that someone appropriate is made aware of any issues that become clear to you. At the K–12 level, that usually means alerting parents or counselors to changes in behavior or academic performance. It can be trickier at the college level, where legal issues may prevent you from contacting others on an adult student's behalf, but you can at least try to encourage the student to seek help.

- *Show empathy.* It's always important to show empathy for your students. Remember that, like you, your students may have a lot going on in their lives outside class. For example, if a student comes to you and says a pet died, realize that this can be a traumatic event, and find a way to give him or her a break for a few days. The same holds true for other personal traumas, whether it is the illness of a relative, parents getting divorced, or a fight with a best friend. In the end, it all comes back to a version of the golden rule: Show your students the same empathy and kindness that you'd like them to show to you. (Of course, you also need to be careful that students don't take improper advantage of your empathy; for example, some students may try to offer excuses when the real problem was simply lack of effort on their part. If necessary, you may need to apply the foreign policy dictum of "trust but verify.")

- *Make your teaching a two-way dialogue.* We should always strive for excellence in teaching, and there's no better way to improve than to get feedback on your current teaching. Feedback from administrators or other teachers is great, but studies by the "Measures of Effective Teaching" project (http://www.metproject.org), sponsored by the Bill & Melinda Gates Foundation, show that your students are uniquely capable of providing outstanding feedback on your teaching. So open a dialogue with your students in which you encourage them to help you improve your teaching just as you seek to help them improve their learning. For example, rather than waiting for end-of-course evaluations (when it's too late for you to do anything for current students), ask students to complete evaluations of your teaching once or a few times during a course; you might even offer an extra-credit point or two for their efforts. You'll be amazed at how much students will tell you (both positive and negative) about your teaching, and if you listen with a critical ear, you'll find these comments will help you become a better teacher. The added benefit — and the reason I've included it in the "be human" category — is that it shows your students that you respect their opinions. And when you show respect to them, they are far more likely to show respect to you.

  NOTE: HOMEWORK EVALUATION Another strategy that I have personally found useful, at least at the college level, is to include a question like the following at the end of each homework assignment: "Please tell me approximately how much time you spent on this assignment. I'd also appreciate any comments (both good and bad) you have about whether you feel the time you spent helped you understand the course material. You may also add any other comments that you think will help me improve as a teacher. Please be honest; your answers will not affect your grade." A significant fraction of my college students would always answer this question. The answers specific to the homework helped me ensure that my homework assignments were of appropriate length and were meeting their pedagogical goals, while more general comments often helped me improve what I was doing in class.

- *"Don't let the turkeys get you down."* No matter how human and empathetic you may try to be, you will still have some students who just won't relate to you and, in some cases, may simply dislike you. While you should certainly make an effort to improve the dynamic in such cases, it may well be beyond your control. So as long as you are doing well with many or most of your students, don't beat yourself up over the rarer ones who can't see your value. Note that this is far easier said than done; for example, those of you who are evaluated by students have probably had the experience of getting a set of almost uniformly good evaluations, but finding yourself sleepless because of a single student who had nasty things to say about you. Why do you let the one bad apple ruin your day? Because you are human, of course. But for your own sanity, you should work to combat this human tendency. And while you should certainly consider whether the negative comments have any grain of truth that might help you improve your teaching in the future, overall you should take more comfort from the positive feedback than consternation from the negative (assuming, of course, that the negative comments are coming from only a small fraction of your students).

6 Seven Pedagogical Strategies for Success in Science Teaching

We now move from general suggestions to more specific strategies that can help you in teaching, particularly in science or other STEM (science, technology, engineering, and mathematics) fields. Before we begin, I'd like to re-emphasize that there's nothing special about the way I've organized these seven strategies; indeed, I've organized them differently in previous incarnations of the talk on which this book is based, and I'm sure you'll notice some overlaps and redundancies in my current organization. So even if you had been so inclined, I hope you won't succumb to any temptation to be like some students who might memorize "Strategy number 4 is…"; instead, I encourage you to focus on the general ideas, and find your own ways to implement them in your teaching.

Strategy 1

Begin with and stay focused on the Big Picture.

Science is filled with interesting facts and details, but your students can absorb them only if they are fit into a "big picture" of the subject matter. It is therefore critical that you begin your course by giving students a big picture overview of what you want them to learn. Then, throughout your course, you should continue to help students fit all the details you cover into that big picture.

A simple example should help make this point clear. We all know that young kids love space, and the more enthusiastic among them can recite a litany of facts about planets, stars, and galaxies. However, you'll find that even the brightest children often interchange the words "solar system" and "galaxy." You might attribute this to a simple slip of the tongue, but with a little probing you'll often discover that the real problem goes much deeper: They have successfully learned lots of individual facts about the solar system

Figure 2. Which one is bigger? Unless they've learned a big picture context, students may have no way to know the answer to this question, let alone that the two objects differ in diameter by a factor of 10 trillion. (Credits: left, NASA/Hubble Space Telescope; right, NASA/Cassini.)

and the galaxy, but are almost completely unaware that the latter is vastly larger than the former. I'm sure you can see that this is a major problem, because it means the kids lack context for their knowledge, which in turn means they probably don't understand any of it very well.

The same is often also true at the high school and college levels. Many students who get As in astronomy or space science classes have learned enough to provide all the answers needed to get high scores on tests, but have missed the big picture of how different levels of structure in the universe relate to one another. If you want to see this problem for yourself (regardless of what subject you are teaching), at the beginning of your term try giving students a question like the one posed in Figure 2. If you are a science teacher, you probably recognize the photo on the left as a galaxy and the photo on the right as a planet (Saturn), which means the one on the left is some 10 trillion times larger in diameter. But how is a student to know this? The two photos appear the same size on the page, and they even have similarity in their disk-like structures and in their orientations as shown. You can probably imagine how a student who doesn't know the answer to this question might still successfully "learn" all kinds of facts about planets and galaxies, and thereby do well on a test despite this major gap in understanding.

NOTE: WE CAN'T EXPECT STUDENTS TO KNOW WHAT THEY HAVEN'T BEEN TAUGHT The case above is also another good example of the fact that we cannot expect students to know what they've never been taught. Astronomy gets relatively little coverage in school these days, so unless students have learned some astronomy on their own, there's a good chance they've never been taught the difference in either appearance or scale between a planet and a galaxy. That's why it is so important to begin by ensuring your students have a big picture context.

Similar examples arise in most any other subject, such as students getting As in high school biology without really understanding evolution, or chemistry and physics students taking the Bohr model of the atom as reality rather than as a tool for calculation, or business students later becoming caught up in market bubbles because they don't understand the basic mathematics governing exponential growth. In all these cases, the students are in essence missing the forest for the trees.

Identifying the Big Picture: In order to stay focused on the big picture, you first need to decide what the big picture consists of for your course. This will vary with level and subject matter, but a good way to start is to make a list of the most important takeaway points that you'd like students to have when they leave your course. I generally recommend that you try to keep the list short, with no more than about three to five big picture goals.

As an example, my big picture goals in teaching astronomy to college nonscience majors are to help students to:

- Understand the nature of science and how science differs from nonscience.
- Build perspective on our place in the universe, both in space and in time.
- Develop a lifelong appreciation of astronomy, so that they will maintain an interest in news reports about astronomy (and other sciences) long after class is over.

In fact, the first and third goals above arguably should apply to *any* science course. The middle goal is more subject specific. For example, in a biology course, you might replace the middle goal with something about understanding the nature and evolution of life, while in physics the middle goal might be for students to understand how we interact with our physical surroundings.

Of course, you may have additional big picture goals. In middle and high school courses, a key big picture goal may be to inspire kids to consider a career in math, science, or engineering, and throughout K–12 education your goals will likely include meeting the Next Generation Science Standards. In college courses for science (or other STEM field) majors, a key goal will be to show students how what they learn now will prepare them for their future coursework or careers.

Opening with the Big Picture: Given how general the big picture goals can be, you may wonder how you actually go about beginning with them. The short answer is the same one I've given for other cases in which there's something you want students to know that they probably don't know already: *just tell them.* If the big picture ideas are really the most important goals for your class (and they should be), then you should tell students this fact up front; there's no point in holding back your big picture ideas like some kind of punch line.

Of course, you also need to explain what your big picture ideas mean. In some sense, you'll spend your entire course doing this, but it's still worthwhile to try to give some explanation up front, meaning in the first couple of weeks of school. To do that, it will be helpful to break your big picture ideas into more teachable components. For example, for my first big picture goal above (understanding the nature of science), I cover some of the historical development of science in the Copernican revolution and discuss the purposes and hallmarks of science (see *What Is Science?*, page 7). I break my second goal above (perspective on our place in the universe) into several components, including an overview of the hierarchy of structure in the universe (e.g., planets, stars, galaxies), putting this hierarchy into context by covering the scale of the universe, and briefly introducing the history of the universe from the Big Bang to the present (along with the associated discussion of the scale of time). Each of those topics can be introduced in one or two class periods, so after about the first two or three weeks of school, I can tell my students that they now have an overview of everything that I really want them to learn in the class, and that the rest of our time will be spent filling in details that should make everything clearer.

NOTE: CHOOSE AN EFFECTIVE ORDER OF PRESENTATION You do not necessarily need to introduce material in the same order that you list your big picture goals. In my astronomy teaching, for example, I've found it more effective to begin with the overview of the universe before discussing the nature of science, because students have no reason to care about the nature of science until you first tell them of some of the amazing things that science has helped us learn about the universe.

NOTE: ON THE LIFELONG LEARNING GOAL In case you're wondering why I didn't break out any components for my third goal (lifelong learning): It's primarily because this is a more general goal that serves primarily to help guide decisions about content coverage; e.g., because we can't cover everything in our limited time, I give preference to topics that students are more likely to see again in their futures than ones that they may never see again (and hence are more likely to forget). Nevertheless, it's still worthwhile to tell students that this is an important goal, and you can support this goal by bringing in news reports to show students that they really will have the opportunity to keep learning about your subject matter for the rest of their lives. You can also provide opportunities for students to see how they will be able to continue study for themselves; in astronomy, for example, observing opportunities will turn some students into lifelong observers of the sky, and a field trip in geology may turn some students into lifelong rock hounds.

Maintaining Focus on the Big Picture: Once you've established the big picture for your students, the next task in this strategy is to *maintain your focus* on the big picture throughout the course. There are two key things you can do to keep this focus:

- First, make sure that all your course material actually connects with your big picture goals; if you find a topic that doesn't seem to fit these goals, then you need to ask yourself whether you should be teaching it at all. If the answer is no, then drop it. If the answer is yes, then see if you can modify your big picture goals to justify inclusion of the topic.

- Second, always take at least a few moments to help your students connect what you are doing on any given day (or on any given assignment) with the big picture goals. Your students will always appreciate knowing that there is a point to what you are asking them to learn, no matter how detailed or complex it may seem when they first encounter it. Or, as one old saying goes: "Tell them what you are going to teach them, teach them, and tell them what you have taught them."

Strategy 2

Always provide context.

We are always more successful in learning something new when we understand its context (and/or relevance). This fact immediately raises one of the primary issues in science teaching: Most students enter our classes with little or no context for the science we are trying to teach them. Therefore, unless we provide that context as part of our teaching, our students will have a difficult time succeeding.

Mental Binning: The idea of context arises on several different levels, so let's start with one of the most basic. Whenever we hear some new fact, our first reaction is to try to fit the fact in with things that we already know. Brain researchers may have some formal way of describing this idea, but I like to think of it in terms of "mental bins." That is, we try to take some new fact and put in into an appropriate mental bin in much the way we might take some document and file it in an appropriate folder on our desktops.

As a simple illustration, imagine that I begin talking to you about "derivatives." If you are a science teacher who learned calculus, you'll immediately prepare to file anything you learn from my talk into the mental bin that represents rates of change. But what if I'm actually talking about derivatives in the financial markets? In that case, unless I tell you up front that financial markets are the context for my talk, you're likely to be very confused until you finally figure out that my talk has nothing to do with calculus.

Many similar difficulties are likely to affect your students. For example, when scientists use the term *theory*, students are likely to place it in a mental bin more closely linked to opinion than to the scientific idea of a model that has been well tested and verified. Some of the examples I've given earlier also illustrate this problem, such as students not understanding that the Sun belongs with the *stars* bin, or taking some fact about a galaxy (such as that it contains lots of dark matter) and applying it to a planet because they don't have different categories of objects properly organized in their heads.

In fact, for much of what we teach in science, the problem goes deeper than students filing information in the wrong mental bins; the problem is that they don't have any pre-existing mental bins in which to fit many of the ideas. There's no reason why students taking their first astronomy course should know what to do when encountering an idea such as the expanding universe, or why students taking their first biology course would know what to do with the idea of viruses or prions. We therefore must help them build the context before we get to the details.

This idea takes us back to Strategy 1, since a big picture overview essentially represents the overarching context for the course. If the big picture does not provide enough context for a particular topic, you should present additional context when introducing the new material. I'll give just a few examples that should show the importance of context; you can probably think of many more from most any field in which you may teach:

Astronomy: Will you grow taller as the universe expands? After learning about the expanding universe, many students incorrectly assume that the answer is yes, because teachers too often leave out the context of expansion as something that can be overcome locally by gravity and other forces. (The correct answer is *no*, because expansion continues only where it has not been locally halted by gravity or some other force. The practical upshot is that the universe expands between galaxies or clusters of galaxies, but galaxies themselves are not expanding, nor are any of the components of galaxies, including stars, planets, and people.)

Biology: How do bacteria acquire resistance to antibiotics? Perhaps as a result of the social pressures put on high school teachers, I've heard of many cases in which students learn the gene transfer mechanisms by which resistance is generally acquired, but do so without learning the crucial context that this is an example of evolution occurring right before our eyes (so to speak).

Geology: Is Earth molten inside? You'd be surprised at how many students think that the entire interior of Earth must be molten, presumably because they learn about volcanoes and mantle convection before anyone first gives them the basic context of Earth's interior structure, or of the fact that solid material can still flow (slowly).

Mathematics: If you put $1,000 in a bank account that is offering 5% interest compounded daily, how much will you have in the account after 10 years? Students will inevitably solve this problem using the compound interest formula, and instructors will almost always expect students to give the answer that pops out of the formula. But do you notice that there are some unstated yet crucial assumptions? For example, where can you find a bank account in which the interest rate will hold perfectly steady for 10 years? What if you have a financial emergency and need to withdraw the money early? Learning to use the compound interest formula is fine and useful, but it will mean much more if you also ensure that students understand the societal context in which a problem like this might actually arise, and what assumptions must hold true in order for the calculated result to be valid.

Climate science: Where does the idea of global warming come from? The topic is often presented to students (and to the public, through the media) as a complex, model-based analysis of recent trends in Earth's climate. But while the atmosphere is indeed complex and climate models are very important as we try to understand the magnitude and consequences of the problem, the underlying physics is very simple — but far too often neglected. As a reminder, the idea of global warming arises from the following simple physical argument:

Fact 1: Carbon dioxide (and other "greenhouse gases") trap heat and make Earth warmer than it would be otherwise. (*How we know*: The heat-trapping effect is directly measurable in the laboratory, and the "make Earth warmer" is a straightforward conclusion from the fact that Earth's calculated temperature based on its distance from the Sun and reflectivity would be below freezing in the absence of greenhouse warming; similar calculations show that other planetary temperatures also make sense only when we include greenhouse warming.)

Fact 2: Human activity such as the burning of fossil fuels (coal, oil, gas) is rapidly increasing the amount of carbon dioxide in Earth's atmosphere. (*How we know*: The rising atmospheric carbon dioxide level has been directly measured since the 1950s, and levels going back nearly a million years can be inferred from ice core data. We can also be sure that the recent increase in carbon dioxide comes from fossil fuels, because the isotopic signature of this carbon dioxide is slightly different from that of carbon dioxide from nonfossil sources.)

Inevitable Conclusion: We should expect the rising carbon dioxide concentration to warm our planet, with the warming becoming more severe as we add more carbon dioxide.

I strongly believe that if we ensured that students and the public always had the above context, the "debate" over the reality of global warming would largely go away, allowing all of us to focus more clearly on how we can address the problem. (For more on this approach to presenting the topic of global warming, please see my post at globalwarmingprimer .com.)

Relevance: A second aspect of context is relevance. It's human nature to be more interested in topics that seem relevant to our daily lives. For that reason, it's always useful to try to connect whatever you are teaching to something that students are likely to care about (besides their grade).

NOTE: RELEVANCE AND CURIOSITY ARE NOT OPPOSED When I present the importance of relevance in my talks, I've occasionally had scientists object that we should encourage curiosity for its own sake. I agree that we should do so, but I don't think this makes it any less important to point out relevance. Those students who are inherently curious about science will not become any less so because you show them the connections between the science and their lives. Meanwhile, those students who come to us without a deep curiosity about science — which is probably rare in elementary school but quite common by college — are much more likely to learn if we show them the relevance; indeed, the relevance may even make them become more curious.

Making material seem relevant is not as difficult as it sounds, because virtually everything in science is relevant to our lives. As a science teacher, you probably recognize this relevance implicitly, so you just need to call it out more explicitly for your students. Again, I'll give you a few examples to show what I mean.

Planetary science/Geology: In these classes, we usually expect students to learn a fair number of facts about other planets. However, while some students think it's cool to learn about Venus or Mars or Jupiter, many other students may wonder why they should care. You can make the other planets relevant by explaining how learning about other planets helps us better understand our own planet Earth (since Earth is surely relevant). For example, show how studies of planetary atmospheres help us understand such things as the greenhouse effect and global warming on Earth, or how comparative geology can help us understand volcanoes and earthquakes, or how Jupiter and other large planets shape the orbits of asteroids and comets that, through impacts, have played a profound role in our planet's history.

Biology: Consider again the teaching of the theory of evolution by natural selection. If it's presented in isolation, some groups of students and parents (and politicians) may think you should avoid teaching it. But if you show how the theory of evolution is in fact the unifying theme of all modern biology, then you will make it relevant to everything you cover, which in turn may help everyone understand why there's no choice about including it in the science curriculum.

Physics/Engineering: Are force diagrams a form of torture? Many students may think so, because these diagrams are often presented context-free. Force diagrams can become much more meaningful if you explain their relevance, which becomes clear if you explain how the diagrams can be useful to, say, building bridges and homes.

Mathematics: To quote Stephen Hawking, "equations are just the boring part of mathematics." So while we obviously need to teach students how to work with equations, they'll be far more motivated to learn if you also show how those equations are useful in practice. In fact, it's worth pointing out that mathematics is necessary in all fields of science and engineering, because the equations provide the way in which we construct models that we can then put to the test, and the verified laws often take a particularly simple form when we write them as equations.

Astronomy: The distant universe may not seem very connected to our daily lives, but I've found that it's easy to show students the relevance of astronomy. The reason is simple: Although we don't always think about it, we all go about our lives with some "world view" shaped by our understanding of (and beliefs about) the universe in which we live. Astronomy informs that world view, and I suspect that it is why most people — and virtually all children — are inherently fascinated by astronomy.

Strategy 3

Emphasize conceptual understanding.

Science has a lot of facts, and it's easy for both teachers and students to fall into a mode in which the main task of a science class becomes the "stamp collecting" of facts. The facts are certainly important, but our real goal should always be to help students build conceptual understanding. After all, individual facts are easily forgotten after a course ends, but a strong conceptual understanding can stay with a student for a lifetime.

It's worth noting that building conceptual understanding is in many ways the aim of all scientific research. The great theories of science are great because they take vast numbers of facts that may otherwise seem disparate and show that they are all offshoots of a single, simple conceptual idea. For example, consider Newton's theory of gravity. Without his theory, the motions of falling objects and the orbital paths of moons and planets would all be separate sets of facts to be learned; with his theory, they are all consequences of a simply stated inverse square law for gravity.

The idea that we should focus on conceptual understanding is nearly universally accepted, yet it is only rarely done well. The best way to improve is simply to think about your teaching and ask yourself whether you are properly focused on the concepts, but I'll offer two specific suggestions that may be of some use.

Use the Concepts to Guide Your Selection of Facts: Much as we discussed with the first two strategies, you can use the idea of conceptual learning to help shape your curriculum. In fact, you can think of the importance of conceptual learning as a third criterion for deciding whether some particular fact or set of facts actually belongs in your course. That is, you should try to make sure that any particular facts you teach meet these three criteria:

1. They are relevant to the big picture.
2. They can be taught with context that will make them meaningful to your students.
3. Knowing these facts will contribute to your students' understanding of some important scientific concept.

If the facts you are thinking about don't meet all three criteria, then your limited time is probably better spent on other topics that will better serve your goals.

NOTE: ON THE NEXT GENERATION SCIENCE STANDARDS For K–12 teachers following the Next Generation Science Standards, much of your selection of facts will be driven by the requirements of the standards. Fortunately, the standards also provide guidance about how to connect the facts to more general scientific and engineering concepts; indeed, this type of context was one of the driving forces behind the new standards. So if you are required to present certain facts, there's probably a good reason for them, which means you can use the three points above as guidelines for how to deliver your content. That is, be sure to show students that the facts tie to your big picture goals, that they have meaningful context, and that they contribute to important scientific concepts.

Simplify but Don't Lie: One of the difficulties of trying to focus on conceptual understanding is that a very deep understanding — the understanding a professional scientist might have — can be quite nuanced and may require knowing and integrating a large number of relevant facts. Clearly, we can't expect students to get such a deep understanding in one year or one course, which means that we must necessarily simplify scientific ideas to make them appropriate to the level at which we are teaching. The need to simplify is perfectly fine in principle, but in practice it often means treading a fairly fine line between "simplifying" and "lying." The former is useful because it can allow students to build their understanding from one course or one year to the next (with increasing levels of complexity over time), while the latter can cause great problems if students one day enter a course in which they are told that something they learned previously was simply not true. Consider the following statements, which I've chosen because they are the type of thing I've often heard teachers say:

"Electrons orbit the nucleus."

"We divide up life into the plant kingdom and animal kingdom."

"There's no friction on ice."

"Evolution makes organisms increasingly complex over time."

Each of these statements represents an attempt to simplify a complex idea, but the simplification has been done in a way that is not strictly correct. For example, there is some friction on ice, and evolution is based on adaptations to local environments and therefore does not always go in the direction of greater complexity. So if you use any statement like the ones above, it's very important to let your students know that the full story is more complex, which you can often do with relatively small changes in the words:

"Electrons go around the nucleus" — and for older students, add: "though you can't really think of them like tiny planets orbiting a sun."

"Most of the life that we see around us is either a plant or an animal" — and for older students, add: "though there are other categories of life (such as mushrooms), and most life is actually microscopic."

"There's very little friction on ice" — and for older students, add a comparison to other sources of friction, such as pavement.

"Evolution means that organisms adapt to their environments over time" — and for older students, explain how this can sometimes increase complexity but sometimes work in the opposite direction.

While these replacement statements are not quite as simple as the originals, they offer two clear benefits: (1) they are true, which means your students won't later be taught something contradictory to what you taught them; and (2) by letting your students know that there's more to the story than you've told them, you inspire them to want to learn more, which hopefully increases their interest in continuing to learn science.

NOTE: THINK OF "EXTRACTING" RATHER THAN "SIMPLIFYING" The most difficult part of "simplify but don't lie" is finding a way to simplify a complex concept without distorting the facts that lie behind it. To help in doing this, I have found it useful to think of "extracting" the key points in a complex topic rather than of "simplifying" the topic. In other words, start by making a list (mental or written) of the most important aspects of a concept you are trying to teach, then present those aspects that are appropriate to the level at which you are teaching. Because you've essentially extracted a subset of the ideas that underlie the concept, there's less risk of saying something untrue than there is if you try to "simplify" a broader range of ideas from the concept. As a case in point, look at my first statement above (about electrons): In replacing "orbit" with "go around," I change the statement from one that has a particular meaning (because orbital paths have distinct shapes) to a much more vague statement that is more difficult to claim as "wrong."

Beware of the Pressures of Testing: Here's a simple fact: It's easier to test a fact than a concept. As we discussed earlier, this explains why most tests — including the increasingly common standardized tests — tend to be heavier on testing facts than on testing conceptual understanding. Indeed, those of us who have made the effort to write tests that focus on conceptual understanding are painfully aware of how great a challenge it is, and hence aware of the limitations of most any test we can give to students. The situation is only marginally better for other types of assignments, including homework and even long essays. The problem is that even when students prove capable of saying all the right things about some concept, it's very difficult to know if they really understand it or if they are just good at telling us what we want to hear.

Please don't take any of this to mean that I'm against testing in general or standardized tests in particular; I strongly believe that both have an important role in education. But this role makes it all the more critical that we bear in mind their limitations. If we succumb to the pressure to teach only to the tests, then we will almost inevitably end up focusing on the stamp collecting of facts at the expense of conceptual understanding.

So… given the limitations of tests, how do we maintain a focus on conceptual understanding? You probably won't be surprised to hear my answer: *make sure your students study.* The fact that learning requires effort and study is especially true for the deep conceptual ideas of science. We may never know for sure if our students have truly grasped some concept, but we can be very confident that they won't grasp it if they haven't studied.

► **K–12 Education**: Some of you may be aware of a recent movement in K–12 education to change grading policies to focus on student "mastery of course material." The understandable motivation for this movement comes from the idea that many schools have allowed students to pass courses based only on effort, rather than on whether they actually understand the material. Unfortunately, as these types of movements often do, this one has swung the pendulum too far to the other side. Many schools implementing these mastery policies are putting essentially all of their grading weight on tests, which means they tend not to assess homework, writing projects, and other assignments that require outside study — and while it's certainly not necessary (or even useful) to give a grade on all assignments, students are far less likely to complete their assignments without some type of assessment or feedback. All this might be fine if the tests actually measured mastery, since in that case you would not be able to pass the tests without really learning the conceptual material. But as we've discussed, it's unrealistic to expect tests to measure true mastery. What we need is a balanced approach: Use well-written tests as an important component of learning and of course grades, but also make sure we still put enough weight on other components to force students to spend time studying. We still can't *guarantee* mastery, but at least we'll know that those students who perform masterfully on tests will have also put in the effort that's required to understand scientific concepts.

▸ **College Education**: At the risk of continuing to beat a dead horse, I see a similar problem in the movement toward reforming the way class time is used in college, particularly for introductory science courses. Again, I see great value in the many reforms to the traditional lecture that have come about in recent years, including the use of clickers, of "think-pair-share" activities, of "lecture tutorials," and more. But for all their benefits, students still need to do their outside studying if we hope for them to build true conceptual understanding. So by all means make use of the new educational reforms, but don't forget that long-term success will still be dictated to a much greater extent by whether you succeed in getting your students to study sufficiently and efficiently.

Strategy 4

Proceed from the more familiar and concrete to the less familiar and abstract.

Consider two ways of teaching Newton's laws of motion. The first way is to present the three laws as fundamental ideas of nature, and then to show students specific examples of how they work. The second is to show students specific examples of the laws in action, then generalize from the examples to the laws. The two approaches may sound very similar, but here's my claim: The first approach is much more common, but everything we know about the human brain and human learning tells us that the second approach is better, because it starts with concrete examples before proceeding to the abstract generalization.

You can see the value of proceeding from the concrete to the abstract, rather than vice versa, in many different ways. For example, the history of science clearly progresses in this way, as an accumulation of concrete discoveries eventually leads someone to put together a theory that explains them. You can probably also see it in your own approach to learning, which I'll illustrate with a simple mathematical example: Suppose you forget whether some particular type of operation is valid, such as whether it is legitimate to square both sides of an equation. Do you set about trying to write a proof to show the operation's validity, or do you simply test a few concrete examples and see if they work? You almost certainly do the latter, which means you are taking concrete examples and generalizing them to an abstract rule.

Perhaps most convincing of all, experiments first conducted more than a half century ago by famed psychologist Jean Piaget showed conclusively that children can reason with concrete ideas before they are able to reason abstractly. When you combine this fact with my earlier claim that "brains are brains," I see no way around the conclusion that *we always learn more easily when we move from concrete to abstract* than the other way around.

"Bridges to the Familiar": One difficulty that we encounter with the concrete-to-abstract idea in science teaching is that many scientific ideas are built upon multiple layers of abstraction, which can make them difficult to tie back to something concrete. For example, the scale of the universe is so vast that it's hard to find ways to describe it concretely; similarly, quantum mechanics builds upon ideas of atoms and small scales that are also very abstract. A good way to deal with this problem is to provide your students with what my friend Jeff Goldstein (of the National Center for Earth and Space Science Education [ncesse.org]) calls "bridges to the familiar." In other words, no matter how abstract some idea may be, try to find some way to link it to a more familiar idea.

I'll give you one of my favorite examples of building a bridge to the familiar. The scale of a galaxy is an important concept in astronomy, and one way to think of it is in terms of the typical number of stars in a galaxy like our own Milky Way, which is on the order of 100 billion. The problem is that this number is so large that students cannot possibly have any concrete experience with it. One way of building a bridge to the familiar in this case is by asking a question like this one: "Suppose you're having trouble falling asleep tonight, and instead of counting sheep you decide to count stars. How long will it take to count 100 billion of them?" If we assume a counting rate of 1 per second, then the answer is 100 billion seconds — which is equivalent to more than 3,000 years. While 3,000 years is still a long time, it's familiar within the context of human civilization and in comparison to our own much shorter lifetimes. The counting question therefore offers students a much more concrete way to understand the number of stars in the galaxy than they can get from just hearing the abstract-sounding number of 100 billion.

NOTE: THE COUNTING EXAMPLE WITH ELEMENTARY STUDENTS A fun and educationally useful way to present the above idea to older students (or the public) is to tell the story of what happens when you give the counting question to elementary school children (and if you are an elementary teacher, you can actually give the question to them). The kids will almost inevitably tell you that they can count much faster than 1 per second, and demonstrate it for you by rattling off the numbers 1 through 10 as fast as they can. Good, you can tell them, but what happens when you get to, say, "thirty-seven billion, four hundred ninety-two million, six hundred eighteen thousand, two hundred forty-four"? Can you still say it in just one second *and* remember what comes next? Note that besides being a cute story that students can appreciate at any age, the story itself is a bridge to the familiar, because it takes the concept you are teaching (the scale of the galaxy) and relates it to something that virtually everyone will remember from childhood (showing how fast you can count).

Context-Driven versus Content-Driven Teaching: We can tie the concrete-to-abstract idea back to our earlier strategy of emphasizing the importance of context in a way that will hopefully give you a concrete way to think about your teaching. I like to think of it as a contrast between two basic approaches to teaching.

Most science (and math) teaching today takes what I call a *content-driven* approach. In other words, we begin by deciding what content we want our students to learn, and then we teach that content, providing specific examples only after we introduce the key content. This is the approach I noted earlier for Newton's laws, in which we start by teaching the laws and then offer examples. Since I spend a lot of my own time on math teaching, I'll note that this approach is even more prevalent in mathematics. For example, in the standard mathematics progression, we almost always teach students the general exponential function before we show them its applications to things like compound interest.

Again, I think this is backwards. What we really want is a *context-driven* approach. We should start by identifying our big picture goals and the context for the material that we want to teach, and then give concrete examples to support that context. Only after that should we generalize to the more abstract content ideas. In the case of Newton's laws, this means first doing the demonstrations and the examples from everyday life before showing how these examples lead you to the laws themselves. In the case of the exponential function, you'll find that students are much more likely to relate to and understand the function when we first use it for compound interest, and only later generalize it to all cases.

As one further example, consider the law of conservation of angular momentum. In a content-driven approach, we present the law and perhaps even show how we derive it from Newton's laws, and then show examples such as ice skaters, spinning bicycle wheels, and gravitationally contracting gas clouds in space. In the context-driven approach we start with the examples, and then show how the same general law applies to all of them; moreover, if the course goals support it, we can then show how the law can be derived from Newton's laws.

Note that, in the end, a context-driven approach allows us to cover the same abstract material as a content-driven approach. The difference is that by starting with context and proceeding from the concrete to the abstract, we're likely to find a much higher proportion of students sticking with us and understanding what we are trying to teach.

Strategy 5

Recognize and address student misconceptions.

Students do not enter our courses as blank slates. Particularly at higher levels, such as high school and college, students often enter our courses not only lacking much understanding of science, but holding misconceptions that can get in the way of anything we hope to teach them. If we hope to be successful in teaching real science, we must first dispel the misconceptions that students bring to us.

Seven Pedagogical Strategies

Note that this strategy therefore has two parts. First, we must *recognize* the misconceptions that students bring. Then we must find an effective way to *dispel* the misconceptions. Let's look briefly at each.

Recognizing Misconceptions: It's not always easy to recognize misconceptions, and many are much more prevalent than we might have guessed. Fortunately, education researchers have by now identified a great many of the most common misconceptions, which means that if you follow educational research, you'll know what to be on the lookout for in your own students. (And if you don't follow the research closely, you should at least check with colleagues to learn about the known misconceptions in any course that you are about to teach.)

Dispelling Misconceptions: It's one thing to tell students that they hold a misconception, and another thing altogether to get them to believe that there's anything wrong with what they think. This is simple human nature: They probably acquired their misconception from experience or being taught incorrectly in the past, possibly by someone in whom they had great trust. If you simply tell them that their conception is wrong, their natural reaction will be to wonder why they should believe *you* over their past experience or teachers.

In fact, I believe that the only way you can successfully dispel misconceptions is by getting students to recognize the misconceptions for themselves. In other words, you need to get them to realize that their thinking does not agree with reality. Sometimes you can do this with demonstrations. Here's a simple example: If you ask students why a rock falls to the ground faster than a piece of paper, most of them (particularly at the elementary and middle school levels) will say that it is because the rock is heavier. You can dispel this misconception simply by balling up the piece of paper and then dropping it with the rock again, since balling it up will remove most of the air resistance and allow the paper to hit the ground at essentially the same time as the rock.

NOTE: AGE EFFECTIVENESS OF THE PAPER-AND-ROCK DEMONSTRATION

The paper-and-rock demonstration will not work for kids below about grade 3, because they have not yet developed what psychologist Jean Piaget called a sense of "conservation." In this case, the problem is that younger kids will not necessarily understand that the process of balling up the paper leaves its weight unchanged; without that realization, the demonstration loses its meaning.

NOTE: EGGS ON THE EQUINOX I can't resist mentioning another favorite
example of using a demonstration to dispel a misconception, this one
the common belief that you can stand an egg on its end only on the
spring equinox. You can, of course, spend time talking about how the
belief makes no sense whatsoever, but the best way to dispel it is to
demonstrate that you can stand an egg on its end on any day of the
year. To see a video proving it, or to learn the technique for yourself,
simply visit Phil Plait's "Bad Astronomy" blog and search for "egg on
equinox." Note that this can be a particularly fun activity with younger
students as they seek to disprove the misconception for themselves.

In other cases, I've found that an effective strategy is to create what I
call "personal paradoxes," in which you get students to see that their prior
beliefs are in some way self-contradictory. Because they are illustrative, I'll
give you three of the most common examples from astronomy, which I
hope will be useful to you as models no matter what subject you teach.

- **Seasons**. One of the most famous astronomical misconceptions was
  popularized by the classic documentary *A Private Universe*, in which
  even Harvard graduates were shown to think that we have summer when
  Earth is closer to the Sun and winter when Earth is farther from the Sun.

  NOTE: AT LEAST THEY KNEW SOMETHING Personally, I don't find the
  Private Universe result all that appalling; rather, I see it as a typical
  example of "we can't expect students to know what they've never
  been taught," since at the time the movie was made, most kids never
  were taught about the real cause of the seasons. In fact, given that
  they had no reason to know the real cause, their answer at least
  demonstrated some decent physical intuition of heat flux, since they
  recognized that we'd expect more heat when closer to the Sun than
  when farther away.

  Dispelling this misconception requires finding a way to get students to
  recognize for themselves that distance from the Sun is *not* the cause of
  the seasons. In many cases you can do this simply by asking the question, "What season is it now in the Southern Hemisphere?" Most high
  school and college students are aware that the seasons are opposite in
  the two hemispheres, so as long as they also recognize that the entire
  Earth is essentially at the same distance from the Sun at any given time,
  then they will recognize that the opposite seasons cannot be explained
  by Earth's varying distance from the Sun. In other words, they'll face a
  personal paradox in which their answer about the seasons conflicts with

Figure 3. You can often dispel the seasons misconception simply by getting students to recognize that the fact that the seasons are opposite in the Northern and Southern hemispheres is inconsistent with the idea that seasons depend on distance from the Sun. However, this works only if students also recognize that our entire planet is essentially at the same distance from the Sun. Unfortunately, there's really no way to draw a correctly scaled diagram of how axis tilt causes seasons; as a result, all seasons diagrams (including the one above) necessarily show Earth magnified so greatly that it ends up looking, for example, like the Northern Hemisphere is closer to the Sun in June than the Southern Hemisphere. This is one more reason why big picture ideas of scale are so important; only if students already understand the real scale will they understand the exaggeration shown in this diagram. (This diagram is extracted from a larger figure in my astronomy textbook series, *The Cosmic Perspective*; the larger figure explains the scale ideas in detail.)

their knowledge that it's summer in Australia when it's winter in the United States. Once they face this paradox, they are much more willing to accept that their original answer could not be correct, and thereby are prepared to listen as you teach them the *real* cause of the seasons in terms of axis tilt.

NOTE: THE IMPORTANCE OF SCALE These days, most kids *are* taught the real cause of the seasons in elementary school, yet the misconception often persists. I believe that a major reason is traceable to the fact that students still are not usually taught about scale. As a result, when they see a diagram of how the seasons work, such as the one in Figure 3, it looks to them like one hemisphere is significantly closer to the Sun than the other at any given moment. This is why I place such great weight on teaching about scale, because only if they've seen what the Sun, Earth, and Earth's orbit look like to scale can they really understand that the entire Earth is essentially at the same distance from the Sun at any given moment. (Using the *Voyage* scale of 1 to 10 billion: The Sun is the size of a large grapefruit, while Earth is smaller than the ballpoint in a pen and orbits at a distance of 15 meters from the grapefruit; viewed this way, any difference in the distance of the two hemispheres is clearly negligible.) In fact, I believe that ideas of scale are crucial not only in astronomy, but also in almost every other science. After all, without a well-developed sense of scale, the microscopic, macroscopic, and astronomical can all become confused.

• **Weightlessness.** If you teach high school or college science, try this one with your students (it sometimes works with younger students as well): First ask, "Why are astronauts weightless in the Space Station?" Most of them will probably answer, "Because there's no gravity in space." Now, follow with "Why does the Moon orbit the Earth?" The students will begin to say, "Because of gravi…" — at which point the good students will stop and you'll literally see their jaws drop as they realize that they are about to give you an answer that directly contradicts the one they gave you a few seconds before. You've created the personal paradox, and because the students will recognize that gravity really is the explanation for the Moon's orbit around Earth, they'll know that their first answer must have been incorrect, which means they are ready to learn the real reason for the weightlessness of the astronauts: Orbit represents a continual state of freefall, and you are always weightless during freefall. (Figure 4 explains why freefall makes you weightless, and Figure 5 shows why orbit is a continuous state of freefall.)

> **NOTE: WHY I DON'T SAY "MICROGRAVITY"** I need to take a moment to get on my soapbox and rant about NASA's poor choice of words in referring to the environment on the International Space Station (or other vehicles in low-Earth orbit) as "microgravity." There is nothing "micro" about the gravity in low-Earth orbit, as a simple computation shows that little g (the acceleration of gravity) is only about 10% smaller in low-Earth orbit than it is on the ground. What NASA means by microgravity is the cumulative effects of all the tiny accelerations that affect any orbiting spacecraft (from causes that include tidal forces), which means they would be better termed "microaccelerations." But from a pedagogical point of view, this is still pointless: For most practical purposes the accelerations are small enough that the astronauts really do feel weightless, so let's just call it that. (And if you are truly a stickler for precision, then I can live with "near weightlessness," but "microgravity" has got to go.)

> **NOTE: ON "APPARENT" VS. "TRUE" WEIGHT** I also need to make a note for the physicists, since most low-level physics textbooks refer to the

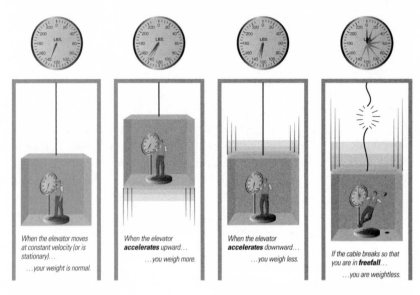

When the elevator moves at constant velocity (or is stationary)... ...your weight is normal.

When the elevator **accelerates** upward... ...you weigh more.

When the elevator **accelerates** downward... ...you weigh less.

If the cable breaks so that you are in **freefall**... ...you are weightless.

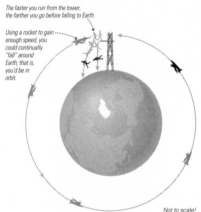

The faster you run from the tower, the farther you go before falling to Earth.

Using a rocket to gain enough speed, you could continually "fall" around Earth; that is, you'd be in orbit.

Not to scale!

Figure 4. (Above) Virtually everyone has ridden an elevator, so the elevator diagram provides a concrete example of varying weight. Students can therefore understand that if the elevator cable broke, you'd lose contact with the scale, which by definition makes you weightless.

Figure 5. (Left) The classic cannonball diagram, adapted to rockets, explains why orbit is a continuous state of freefall. (Both figures are from my astronomy textbook series, *The Cosmic Perspective*.)

changes that occur in an elevator (Figure 4) as changes in "apparent weight," rather than in true weight; they define the latter as *mg* (mass times the acceleration of gravity). The problem is that while this distinction works fine for elevators on Earth, it becomes ambiguous for cases such as a spacecraft on its way to the Moon, because it's no longer clear what value should be used for *g*. Moreover, in astronomy we eventually need to teach our students at least something about

Figure 6. The flag in scenes from the Apollo missions has unfortunately fed the common misconception that there's "no gravity on the Moon." You can dispel this misconception with a personal paradox when you get students to realize that the astronauts and spacecraft must be on the ground due to gravity, since without gravity they'd be floating off. (This painting of the *Apollo 11* scene is from my children's book *Max Goes to the Moon.*)

general relativity, so that they can understand ideas such as why the universe does not have a center and edges. In general relativity, the distinction between apparent weight and true weight becomes meaningless, because weight (or lack of it) is determined by the nature of an object's worldline.

- **Gravity on the Moon.** A closely related misconception was inadvertently fed by the fact that NASA chose to use a telescoping pole to hold up the flags that the Apollo astronauts took to the Moon. The photos of these flags have led many people to believe that there's "no gravity on the Moon." Because it's so much fun, I'll tell you how I set up the situation for the personal paradox with elementary school kids. (You can use the same personal paradox for older students, but they may not appreciate the humor in the same way as the younger kids.)

I begin by showing a painting of the *Apollo 11* scene (Figure 6); to make sure I get the answer I'm looking for, I phrase the first question as follows: "If you look closely, you'll notice that the flag looks like it's doing something that it should *not* be doing on the Moon; who can tell me what that is?" Somewhat remarkably, I've found that even most kindergartners will correctly answer that the flag looks like it's blowing in the wind, but it can't be because there's no air or wind on the Moon. (It's remarkable in that I find it amazing that kids as young as kindergartners already know that the Moon is airless, something that certainly is not obvious from looking at it in the sky.)

"Good," I tell them, "but then why is the flag staying up?" As they raise their hands, I say, "You can put your hands down, because even though I'm sure a lot of you know the right answer, I want to tell you the *wrong* answer."

This inevitably draws sounds of surprise, at which point I explain: "Now, you're probably wondering why I'm going to tell you the wrong answer instead of the right one. Well, it's a little embarrassing but… [in a whisper] it turns out that it's what a lot of grownups say… [regular voice] It's so silly you'll probably burst out laughing, but lots of grownups try to say the flag stays up because 'there's no gravity on the Moon.'"

The kids will inevitably laugh at this point, which means I can now bring in the personal paradox: "I told you it was silly. After all, you can tell that there *is* gravity on the Moon just by looking at the picture. Who can tell me how?" At this point, almost all of the kids will answer correctly, stating that the astronauts and the spacecraft both show clearly that there's gravity, because they're not floating away. To close, I circle back to the flag, and explain that without support, it would be hanging straight down.

NOTE: IT'S A SUPER-BOWL-CLASS MISCONCEPTION In case you're wondering how prevalent this misconception really is, it appeared in a particularly egregious way in a Super Bowl commercial run by FedEx a few years ago (2007). The commercial (which you may still find with a search on "FedEx Super Bowl XLI commercial") showed people in an office on the Moon — with FedEx delivery — with some of them floating (including a dog!), some of them bouncing, and some of them walking as though in normal Earth gravity. We can only assume that the people who worked on and approved the multimillion-dollar ad were themselves very confused about gravity on the Moon. (The ad also featured a meteor of some sort blazing a visible trail as it came in toward the Moon, which is also impossible because the Moon's lack of atmosphere means that incoming particles do not leave visible trails.)

NOTE: HEAVY BOOTS There's also a terrific (possibly apocryphal) story about this misconception in which a philosophy teaching assistant claims that a pen would float away if you dropped it on the Moon; when asked why the Apollo astronauts didn't float away, he replies, "Because they were wearing heavy boots." The story is posted on numerous web sites (try a search on "heavy boots on the Moon"), but I have not been able to track down its original source.

Simple demonstrations and personal paradoxes are particularly good ways to dispel misconceptions, but they are not always possible. In such cases, you'll need to find some other way to get students to recognize the errors in their thinking for themselves. Sometimes it's just a matter of asking students to think about whether some idea really makes sense. My astronomy textbook co-author Megan Donahue tells a story about growing up in Nebraska and being told that the sky is blue because of reflection from the oceans, which clearly didn't make sense for such a deep inland location. A common misconception requiring an extra step is the well-known one in which students think that moon phases are caused by shadows from Earth. To dispel this one, you first have to get students to realize that the Moon orbits Earth. Once you do that, you can show how most positions in the orbit mean that no shadow from Earth could possibly hit the Moon, at which point you can begin to talk about (and demonstrate) the real cause of the phases.

Not all misconceptions are as easy to dispel as the ones I've given as examples here, but the bottom line should be clear: Unless you first dispel a student's misconceptions, there's little chance that you'll be able to teach that student a correct understanding.

Strategy 6

Use plain language.

Open up an introductory college science textbook and start counting the number of bold or glossary terms that are likely to be unfamiliar to students when they first enroll in a class. Although there is a large range, most college-level textbooks have a least several hundred such terms, and some (particularly in biology) have upwards of 1,500. Amazingly, this turns out to be *comparable to or greater than the number of vocabulary words that students typically learn in a first-year foreign language course.* Given that most students find science itself to be unfamiliar, the large amount of jargon clearly makes their task of learning it far more difficult. In essence, it's as though we are attempting to teach introductory students an unfamiliar subject (science) in what to them sounds like a foreign language. The situation in K–12 education is only marginally less severe.

If all this jargon were helpful to conceptual understanding, then we might be justified in expecting students to learn it. But while some jargon is clearly necessary, in many cases we use jargon that no one besides specialists in a particular scientific discipline ever really needs to know. For an astronomical example, ask yourself whether you could identify:

- *scarps* on Mercury
- *lunar regolith*
- the distinction between *chondrites* and *achondrites*

The italicized terms are all commonly found in astronomy textbooks intended for nonscience majors, yet few people besides planetary geologists have any idea what they mean. Indeed, when I have presented these terms in talks to college astronomy faculty, many of whom have taught out of textbooks that use these terms, I've still found it rare to find anyone who knows all of them. Given that most professional astronomers don't even know what these terms mean, why would we ever expect nonmajor freshman or high school students to learn them?

In the vast majority of cases, replacing jargon with plain language has no downside and a tremendous upside in making it easier for students to focus on real scientific concepts. The only exceptions are when the jargon has entered the common vernacular, so that students are likely to hear the same terminology in news reports, and when you are teaching upper-level students who need to become conversant in the language of their discipline. With that in mind, I'll offer a few suggestions on dealing with different types of jargon, along with examples of each. I apologize in advance for giving many more examples here than in the rest of the strategies, but I think they are particularly illustrative in this case.

NOTE: JARGON REDUCTION IS *NOT* "DUMBING DOWN" Back in the section on the one key to student success, I noted the pressure to lower expectations and dumb down courses and textbooks. Some of you may wonder if the idea of reducing jargon is an example of this very type of dumbing down. My answer is no, because I don't believe that the jargon serves to enhance understanding. In fact, I believe that reducing jargon actually allows us to *raise* expectations, because by removing the foreign language aspect we have more time available to cover the breadth and depth of the scientific subject matter. Also worth noting: Students and others often use jargon to try to give people the impression they know more than they do; reducing jargon can therefore expose how much or little is truly understood.

NOTE: PLEASE "DNUA" Do you know what I mean when I say "DNUA"? (And how do you pronounce it?) Probably not, because I just made it up: It's my new acronym for "Do Not Use Acronyms." The fact is, acronyms are rarely helpful, because unless they are among the rare ones that have made it into the common vernacular (such as radar, laser, or NASA), they are just another form of jargon that students have to learn — and in the case of acronyms, they are easily replaced by writing the words out. Sure, it takes a little more typing or a little more breath for me to say "do not use acronyms" than it does for me to say "DNUA," but that's a small price to pay for making sure that you'll know what I'm talking about. The same is true for virtually all other acronyms. So as part of your general jargon reduction effort, please reduce your use of acronyms. The closer you can get to zero use, the better. And when you just can't avoid them — for example, you'll find numerous places in this book where I've used the acronym STEM (science, technology, engineering, and mathematics) — at least put the full term in parentheses once in a while, so as to remind students of what you mean.

Translate When Possible: In many cases, the jargon we use in science can be translated simply into plain language, which is exactly what you should do in those cases. Consider the three terms I gave you above, but now with translations:

- *Scarps* are just a fancy name that planetary geologists like to use for the long, tall cliffs that are prevalent on Mercury.

  NOTE: A TRUE STORY Once when I gave my talk to a faculty group that included several geologists, one of the geologists took exception to my translation, explaining that scarps are not really quite the same as cliffs. Another geologist then stood up and said that he agreed they were not quite the same, but disagreed with the first geologist on the reason. A third then stood up and said that actually, he thought of them as synonymous. The debate continued for several minutes, by which time I think they all agreed that whatever the distinction might or might not be, it was not something that freshman non-majors needed to know.

Figure 7. Familiar photos of astronaut footprints make it clear that the Moon's surface is covered by a powdery soil. Telling students that this powdery soil is technically called the lunar regolith does not in any way enhance their understanding of the lunar surface; in fact, it reduces their understanding by forcing them to learn an unnecessary term that they're almost guaranteed to forget later anyway. (NASA, *Apollo 11*)

- *Lunar regolith* is a fancy name for the powdery lunar soil in which the astronauts left their footprints (Figure 7).

- *Chondrites* and *achondrites* are types of meteorite. The names describe a particular geological characteristic (the presence or absence of small, round *chondrules*), but the former are thought to represent primitive material that condensed in the very beginning of the solar system's history, while the latter represent meteorites that were once pieces of larger asteroids (either pieces chipped off an asteroid's surface in an impact or remnants of an asteroid that shattered in a collision) and that therefore have undergone geological processing since the solar system first formed. Given all that, it's much simpler to refer to the chondrites as "primitive meteorites" and the achondrites as "processed meteorites," since those terms directly reflect the differences between them.

Before we move on to the next jargon type, it's worth thinking about what happens if you *don't* use simple translations when they are available. Just as it takes years to become fluent in a foreign language, it takes years to become totally comfortable with scientific jargon. During the short time you have students in your class, even those who memorize the meaning of a piece of jargon will inevitably go through a mental translation every time they hear it. For example, every time you say "scarp," the student will need to pause and recall that it means "cliff" — and during that mental pause, they may miss something else important that you were trying to teach them.

Seek Simpler Choices: Translations like those above are available only when a term has a direct counterpart in plain language. In science, there are many cases in which a word goes with a concept that is likely to be unfamiliar, which means you won't find a direct translation. Nevertheless, there are often choices of available jargon in such cases, and you should always seek the simpler choices. Again, I'll offer some astronomical examples, and I'm sure you can find similar examples in whatever subject you teach.

- Professional astronomers often measure distances to stars in units called *parsecs* and distances to galaxies in *megaparsecs*. But these can be easily converted into *light-years* and *millions of light-years*, respectively, because 1 parsec = 3.26 light-years. Light-years are still a form of jargon since they are not a familiar unit from everyday life, but the name itself helps explain what the unit means (it is the *distance* that light travels in one year through empty space, which is roughly 10 trillion kilometers, or 6 trillion miles). In contrast, the term *parsec* is utterly meaningless to most people, which makes it a less desirable choice of jargon. (In case you are wondering, the term *parsec* is short for "parallax second," and it is geometrically defined as the distance at which an object would have an annual parallax shift in our sky of one arcsecond.)

    NOTE: PAY ATTENTION TO JARGON IN THE MEDIA This particular example is illustrative of how the common vernacular can come into play. Until a little more than a decade ago, virtually all astronomers quoted Hubble's constant in units of kilometers per second per megaparsec, and as a result, those were the units that you generally saw in news sources such as *The New York Times*. That has since changed, however, and news sources now usually ask scientists to give Hubble's constant in units of kilometers per second per million light-years. So while teaching nonmajor students the jargon of parsecs and megaparsecs may have been justifiable when they were likely to see it in the media, there's no longer any good reason for them to learn the terms.

- Traditionally, the balance between gravity and pressure in a stable astronomical object has been called *hydrostatic equilibrium*. (The term is also used for Earth's atmosphere and for other fluids.) But this term confuses students a great deal, because it has nothing to do with any of the mental bins in which they are likely to try to fit it, such as those for water, hydrogen, or static electricity. A number of years ago, a couple of prominent astronomers wrote a book in which they replaced the term "hydrostatic equilibrium" with the term *gravitational equilibrium* (Begelman, Mitchell and Rees, Martin, *Gravity's Fatal Attraction*, Scientific American

Library, 1996). It's still a form of jargon, but note how much easier it is to remember that gravitational equilibrium is a balance between gravity and pressure. Indeed, it has an added advantage: The standard jargon for what happens to a star as it shrinks due to its own gravity is *gravitational contraction*, so it makes perfect sense to think that once gravity is offset by pressure, the star settles into a state of gravitational equilibrium.

- In the first edition of Taylor and Wheeler's classic textbook on relativity, called *Spacetime Physics*, there was a lot of discussion of *inertial reference frames*. In the second edition, that term was replaced by *free-float frames*. Again, the new term is still a form of jargon, but it has an underlying sense to it; after all, the defining characteristic of an inertial reference frame is that it is a reference frame in which you would float freely.

  NOTE: WHEN JARGON IS UNAVOIDABLE, POINT OUT WORD ROOTS AND ETYMOLOGY The Latin origin of the term *inertia* (which means "inactivity") reminds me that while I'd like to see this particular term discarded, there are other cases in which jargon is unavoidable, and in those cases we can often help students by pointing out its roots or etymology. A couple of simple examples from biology: (1) The structures in the ear called *scala* get that name because *scala* means "ladders," and they look somewhat like ladders. (2) The term *phage* comes from a word meaning "glutton" or "eater," which helps explain why a *bacteriophage* is not itself a bacterium but rather a virus that infects (and often kills) bacteria.

- Professional astronomers talk about different types of supernovae as Type I or Type II, with the first category further subdivided into Types Ia, Ib, and Ic. The types have historical pedigree in describing characteristics of different supernova spectra, but today we think we have a pretty good understanding of supernovae. This understanding tells us that they come in two basic types: a type that occurs when a high-mass star explodes and a type that occurs when a white dwarf (an object that is the remains of a low-mass star that has died) explodes. So why not just call the two types "massive star supernovae" and "white dwarf supernovae?" It's much easier than trying to remember the correspondence to the "types," especially since that correspondence turns out to be complex: Type Ia supernovae are the only ones thought to be from white dwarfs, which means that Types Ib, Ic, and II all represent essentially the same type of progenitor.

NOTE: PLEASE DON'T "TYPE"-CAST SCIENCE I'll go further and give you a general rule about "types": The terms "Type I" and "Type II" are so overused throughout science that they can never be helpful to students. For example, depending on your field of study, you may deal with Type I and Type II errors, Type I and Type II ionic compounds, Type I and Type II muscle fibers, Type I and Type II schizophrenia, Type I and Type II diabetes, and even Type I and Type II (and Type III) civilizations!

- As you may notice from my note above about "types," scientists often overuse favorite words. For astronomers, one of these favorites is "dwarf." There are dwarf planets and dwarf galaxies, brown dwarfs, white dwarfs, black dwarfs, red dwarfs, yellow dwarfs, and more. Even worse, most of these different dwarfs have little in common with one another. In a few cases, such as for brown dwarfs (objects that are in between a large planet and a small star) or white dwarfs (which are a type of dead stellar core), there really aren't any alternative terms, so we're stuck with them. But red dwarfs, for example, are ordinary stars that are relatively small in size and red in color. Because we already have a piece of jargon that students learn for ordinary stars — they are called *main-sequence stars* — there's no reason to use the term "red dwarf," since such a star is just as easily and much more clearly described as a "red main-sequence star." (I consider the jargon "main-sequence stars" to be acceptable, both because there's no easy replacement and because it emphasizes an idea that students really do need to learn in astronomy, which is that all such stars form a well-defined sequence when they are plotted on a graph of temperature versus luminosity [the "H–R diagram," another piece of jargon which I'll say more about below].)

NOTE: A DWARF QUIZ Try this question: *What color is a brown dwarf?*

a. brown   c. magenta
b. green   d. dwarfish

This is the first question from a short quiz that I wrote a few years ago, when I became so annoyed by the overuse of the term "dwarfs" that I felt I needed something to show the insanity of this jargon. You may find the full quiz entertaining, so I've included it as Appendix 3. And in case you are wondering, the correct answer to this first question is c (magenta) — really!

It's Nice to Honor Them, But…: Another common form of jargon in science arises from the habit of naming things in honor of their discoverers (or at least the people who first published them). We say "Newton's laws" and expect people to know we mean the laws of motion, or "Kepler's laws" and expect people to know we're talking about planetary motion, or "Maxwell's equations" with the expectation that they'll know we're talking about equations governing electromagnetism, or "Magellanic clouds" and assume they know we're talking about two small galaxies that were known to people in the Southern Hemisphere for millennia before Europeans decided to name them for Magellan. These examples at least involve somewhat famous names, but here are some others you'll find in many introductory astronomy books: Kirchhoff's laws, Herbig-Haro objects, Seyfert galaxies, Zeeman effect, Chandrasekhar limit, Hertzsprung-Russell or H–R diagram, and Oort cloud (which has essentially nothing in common with the Magellanic clouds). None of these names are likely to be familiar to anyone outside of the professional astronomy community.

I suppose it's nice that we like to hand out scientific honors, but learning all these names is as useful to helping students learn science as memorizing state capitals is to helping them understand U.S. history. So while we all probably hope something will be named for us someday, we'll do our students a big favor if we do our best to say what we mean instead of dropping names.

There are some cases in which we are probably stuck with the names because they are so famous, such as with Newton or Kepler or Maxwell, but even then we can try to be clearer by saying, for example, "Newton's laws of motion" (rather than simply "Newton's laws") or "Maxwell's equations of electromagnetism." There are other cases in which there are not yet any widely recognized alternatives; for example, I'm unaware of any easy replacement term for the "Oort cloud," which refers to the vast space around our solar system that is thought to be inhabited by trillions of comets, and the H–R diagram seems an acceptable shorthand for the alternative of having to repeatedly say "a diagram that plots stars by temperature on the horizontal axis and luminosity on the vertical axis." But there are many other cases in which there's an easy work-around; using a few of my earlier examples, the Chandrasekhar limit can be called the "white dwarf limit" (because it is a limit on the mass of a white dwarf), the Zeeman effect can simply be described as the splitting of spectral lines due to a magnetic field, and Kirchhoff's laws are laws describing how spectra form. In these and similar cases, the work-arounds allow students to focus on the concepts rather than on the "stamp collecting" of names.

Be Accurate, But Not Persnickety: Even while we reduce jargon, I still believe it's very important that we be accurate with our terminology in science. For example, we should not allow students to mix up terms like weight and mass, even if they are commonly interchanged in everyday language. Nevertheless, there are cases where complete technical accuracy just adds to the confusion, and in those cases I think we can make reasonable judgments on the side of clarity. Three examples that, while from astronomy, are likely to be familiar to almost everyone:

- What do you call a small rock floating in space that comes crashing down to Earth? Technically, while it's in space, it's a *meteoroid*; on its way down, it becomes a *meteor*; and the remnant piece that hits the ground is called a *meteorite*. But movies and popular culture often call it a "meteor" in all three cases, and is there really any harm in that? Perhaps it's worth a couple sentences in class (or in a textbook) to explain the technical differences to students, but I wouldn't give a test question on it.

- Comets have a similar problem. The word *comet* comes from a Greek word for "hair," which means that an icy object technically becomes a comet only when it is close enough to the Sun for its ices to vaporize and form a tail (the "hair"). For that reason, the objects that become comets are technically *not* called comets when they are far from the Sun, but we sure confuse students when we tell them that an icy object gradually "becomes" a comet as it approaches the Sun (and then stops being one when it returns to being far away from the Sun). Doesn't it make much more sense to refer to all icy objects that could in principle grow tails as comets, no matter whether they are currently frozen and far from the Sun or currently approaching the Sun and forming a tail? An added advantage of this approach is that it means that Pluto is really just a big comet, which is a lot more meaningful than the whole debate about what should be called a planet.

- Speaking of planets, I've been surprised by how much time some teachers spend debating the demotion of Pluto. Nature doesn't always have clear distinctions between categories, and the distinction between "large comet" (or asteroid, if it's rocky), "dwarf planet," and "planet" is not really any more important than the distinction between "creek,"

Seven Pedagogical Strategies

"stream," and "river." Let's spend our time focusing on the science of the solar system, not on battles over naming.

NOTE: WHEN EARTH WASN'T A PLANET It's worth pointing out that the word *planet* has been through several past redefinitions. The word itself comes from the Greek for "wanderer" and the seven planets of ancient times were the seven objects that appear to wander among the constellations — which means that the Sun and Moon were originally considered planets, while Earth was not.

Be Clear When Jargon Conflicts with Common Usage: There are some cases in which scientific jargon actually uses plain-language terms, but with a different meaning than they have in ordinary speech. In those cases, we need to be especially careful to be sure that students understand what we actually mean.

The most notable case is the word *theory*. In everyday speech, the term is often used synonymously with *hypothesis*, but in science the two ideas are very different. After all, when creationists say that evolution is "only a theory," they don't intend to mean the same thing that we mean by a theory in science, which is a broad-based model that successfully explains a vast body of evidence and that has been repeatedly tested and verified. I think the best way to deal with this type of situation is to be very clear in explaining the idea of a scientific theory to students, both when we first introduce it and whenever the term arises in any of our discussions.

NOTE: WHY I STILL LIKE THE TERM "THEORY" A few of my colleagues (most notably, planetary scientist David Morrison) have suggested that the term "theory" is so misunderstood that we should simply avoid it; for example, we could simply refer to "evolution" rather than the "theory of evolution." There is some merit to this idea, but I also see some risks. For example, in helping students understand the nature of science, I think it is important to distinguish between the "observational facts of evolution" — meaning the fossil record with its clear demonstration that evolution occurs — and the "theory of evolution" that describes how evolution proceeds through natural selection. The former is not subject to any scientific debate at all, while the latter is continually being refined as we learn more about the molecular basis of evolution and the precise timing of evolutionary changes. If we simply say "evolution," we lose the ability to make this important distinction.

Similar clarity is needed in cases where jargon tends to evoke misconceptions. For example, the name "theory of relativity" has tended to make people think that it says "everything is relative," when in fact it refers specifically to the relativity of motion. Again, the best defense in this case is to let your students know that it does *not* mean that everything is relative, and then explain what it does mean.

There are many more cases in which we tend to use terms in science with a different meaning than they typically have in everyday life. One of the best lists I've seen of such terms was published in the article "Communicating the Science of Climate Change," by Richard Somerville and Susan Joy Hassol (*Physics Today*, Oct. 2011), which my textbook co-authors and I have modified and expanded into Table 2 on pages 100–101.

Don't Make a Bad Jargon Situation Worse: My final comment on jargon is that, given how bad the jargon situation already is, we should work hard to avoid making it worse. Unfortunately, the pressure tends to work in the opposite direction, because whenever scientists (including those who do research in science education) learn something new, there's a great temptation to assign a piece of jargon to it. In addition, particularly for discoveries that get press coverage, there's often a temptation to make up "cute" new names that may get great media play but that probably don't help student or public understanding. I'll give you a few recent examples of new jargon that really should *not* have been introduced:

- "The God particle." In case you missed it, this is the media-blessed name for the Higgs boson, a subatomic particle whose existence was predicted decades ago (by Peter Higgs) but was only recently confirmed through experiments at the Large Hadron Collider in Europe. But the name "God particle" is truly egregious: Not only is it preposterous to presume that this particle is so important that it equates to God, but the term runs completely counter to our goal of showing the public that science and religion are *not* in conflict. Just call the particle the Higgs boson — it's still a piece of jargon, but the particle has to have some kind of name, and in this case the name "Higgs" is probably as good as any.

- "The Goldilocks zone." This term has recently become popular as a way to describe the region around a star in which an Earth-like planet (e.g., a planet with liquid-water oceans on its surface) could conceivably form. Both scientists and the media now routinely use this term over the formerly favored "habitable zone," presumably because it's kind of cute to

(*continues after Table 2*)

Seven Pedagogical Strategies

Table 2. Scientific Usage Often Differs from Everyday Usage

This table is adapted from the article "Communicating the Science of Climate Change," by Richard Somerville and Susan Joy Hassol (*Physics Today*, Oct. 2011).

Term	Everyday meaning	Scientific meaning	Example
model	something you build, like a model airplane	a representation of nature, sometimes using mathematics or computer simulations, that is intended to explain or predict observed phenomena	A model of planetary motion can be used to calculate exactly where planets should appear in our sky.
hypothesis	a guess or assumption of almost any type	a model that has been proposed to explain some observations, but which has not yet been rigorously confirmed	Scientists hypothesize that the Moon was formed by a giant impact, but there is not enough evidence to be fully confident in this model.
theory	speculation	a particularly powerful model that has been so extensively tested and verified that we have extremely high confidence in its validity	Einstein's theory of relativity successfully explains a broad range of natural phenomena and has passed a great many tests of its validity.
bias	distortion, political motive	tendency toward a particular result	Current techniques for detecting extrasolar planets are biased toward detecting large planets.
critical	really important; involving criticism, often negative	right on the edge	A boiling point is a "critical value" because above that temperature, a liquid will boil away.
deviation	strangeness or unacceptable behavior	change or difference	The recent deviation in global temperatures compared to their long-term average implies that something is heating the planet.

Table 2. (*continued*)

Term	Everyday meaning	Scientific meaning	Example
enhance/ enrich	improve	increase or add more, but not necessarily to make something "better"	"Enhanced color" means color that has been brightened. "Enriched with iron" means containing more iron.
error	mistake	range of uncertainty	The "margin of error" tells us how closely measured values are likely to reflect true values.
negative feedback	poor response	a self-regulating cycle	The Sun's fusion rate is steady because if it were to go up, negative feedback would cause it to go back down.
positive feedback	good response, praise	a self-reinforcing cycle	Gravity can provide positive feedback to a forming planet: Adding mass leads to stronger gravity, which leads to more added mass, and so on.
state (as a noun)	a place or location	a description of current condition	The Sun is in a state of balance, so that it shines steadily.
trick	deception or prank	clever approach	A mathematical trick solved the problem.
uncertainty	ignorance	a range of possible values around some central value	The measured age of our solar system is 4.55 billion years with an uncertainty of 0.02 billion years.
values	ethics, monetary values	numbers or quantities	The speed of light has a measured value of 300,000 km/s.

think of the region in which a planet could be habitable as the "just right" region around a star in the same way that Goldilocks found the baby bear's porridge, chair, and bed to be "just right" in the English fairy tale known as "Goldilocks and the Three Bears." The problem, however, is that not everyone knows the Goldilocks story; in fact, it's rarely known to people whose native language is not English, and often unfamiliar to students with immigrant parents. Given that one of our goals is to increase the diversity of students entering science, it's crazy to introduce a new term that will make no sense to them when we have a perfectly good term (*habitable zone*) already.

- "Ice giants." Recently, some planetary scientists have taken to referring to the planets Uranus and Neptune as "ice giants." Their reasoning is as follows: These planets have traditionally been grouped with Jupiter and Saturn as the "gas giants," a term that makes at least some sense because Jupiter and Saturn are composed primarily of hydrogen and helium, which we usually think of as being gases. However, the compositions of Uranus and Neptune are actually dominated by hydrogen-based compounds such as water (H_2O), methane (CH_4), and ammonia (NH_3) — and these are substances that can be frozen to make ices on Earth (and are ices in comets and on many moons). But here's a simple fact: Except perhaps for some snowlike particles in their clouds, *there is essentially no ice at all* inside either Uranus or Neptune; rather, the high pressures and temperatures in the planetary interiors compress these hydrogen compounds into other phases (some familiar from Earth and some not). So with apologies to my friends who like the term, using the term "ice giant" for planets with virtually no ice at all makes virtually no sense.

    NOTE: SO WHAT SHOULD WE CALL URANUS AND NEPTUNE? While "ice giants" is a terrible term, other options are not all that great either, especially since discoveries of extrasolar planets have shown us that planets come in a wider range of types than we had recognized when we knew only the planets of our own solar system. But until we get a better understanding of planetary types, I'd advocate sticking with what has long been an alternative to "gas giants," which is the term *jovian planets* (*jovian* means "Jupiter-like"). One reason I prefer this term is that just as Uranus and Neptune really don't contain ice, Jupiter and Saturn don't really contain much gas, because the high-pressure conditions found throughout most of their interiors compress the "gases" into liquid, metallic, or other strange forms. But in addition, the term "jovian" can be thought of in terms of planetary formation, and the planets Jupiter, Saturn, Uranus, and Neptune are all thought to have formed in a similar way that is distinct from the way the four terrestrial ("Earth-like") planets formed. (The outer planets are thought to have formed around large "cores" made of ice, rock, and metal that had condensed from the cloud of gas that gave birth to our solar system, and these cores were massive enough for their gravity to then collect some of the abundant hydrogen and helium gas that surrounded them. The differences between Jupiter/Saturn and Uranus/Neptune can then be traced simply to the amounts of the hydrogen and helium they captured.)

- "Flipped classrooms." OK, I'm guilty of having used this one in this book, though you'll notice that I always put it in quotes and defined it clearly when I first introduced it. But the truth is, I used it mainly because I expect that a substantial fraction of the people reading a book like this one will be familiar with it and will expect to see it, not because it's necessarily a good idea. For example, think about the image that this term must evoke when nonteachers hear it: Do they picture a teacher standing in the back of the class instead of the front, or tables and chairs placed upside down, or students hanging from the ceiling? I also dislike the term because it makes it sound like some new idea, but as I pointed out earlier, many great teachers have in essence employed this strategy for a very long time. Personally, I'd advocate simply talking about the value of having students come to class prepared for activities and discussions.

Strategy 7

Challenge your students.

I'll keep this one short, because while it's very important, it's really just a restatement of ideas we've discussed earlier. You are a science teacher because you love science. You undoubtedly find it amazing, fascinating, even awe-inspiring. If you convey your passion for science to your students, they'll love it too. In fact, they'll love it so much that they'll want you to challenge them, and they will rise to meet any reasonable expectations you set for them, as long as you follow the other strategies and practices of good teaching that we've discussed.

With that in mind, be sure that you never dumb your teaching down. Expect excellence, and you're likely to get it. If there's a topic that excites your passion, don't be afraid to share it with your students. Remember, in the long run, the greatest success you can have as a science teacher lies in giving your students a lifelong love of science, along with the tools that they'll need to understand the role of science in modern society (and for science majors, the tools they'll need to succeed in their careers). If you do this, you'll have put your students on a path to helping all of us win the race between education and catastrophe.

7 Putting It All Together

When I'm teaching or writing, I always like to end a class or a chapter with a wrap-up that tries to tie all the big ideas together. It's not meant to be a complete summary, nor is it meant to list all the key ideas (which you can find in the detailed list of headings and notes that begins on page 153). Rather, this wrap-up is meant to be a way of looking back to see how everything we discussed was related to our main goal or goals. In this book, the main goal is to help you improve your own teaching. With that in mind, I think the following three simple ideas should help tie all our other themes together.

- Students need to study to learn. Therefore, your most important job as a teacher is to help your students to make the necessary effort of studying.

- Teaching is an art. There is no single best way to inspire your students to learn, so you must constantly re-evaluate your success in getting students to study sufficiently and efficiently.

- Science is important. We need all students to understand the nature of science and its role in modern society, and to remain engaged with science throughout their lives.

APPENDICES

How to Succeed Handout

The following is the text of a handout I offer to students on how to succeed in college classes. A pdf of this handout is available on the book web site (OnTeachingScience.com), formatted to fit a single sheet of paper (front and back); you can feel free to download it and make use of it in your own classes.

HINTS ON HOW TO SUCCEED IN COLLEGE CLASSES

The Key to Success: Study Time

The single most important key to success in any college course is to spend enough time studying. A rule of thumb is that you should expect to study about 2 to 3 hours per week *outside* of class for each unit of credit. For example, a student taking 15 credit hours should expect to spend 30 to 45 hours each week studying outside of class. Combined with time in class, this works out to a total of 45 to 60 hours spent on academic work—not much more than the time a typical job requires, and you get to choose your own hours. Of course, if you are working while you attend school, you will need to budget your time carefully.

As a rough guideline, your study time might be divided as shown in the table below. If you find that you are spending fewer hours than these guidelines suggest, you can probably improve your grade by studying longer. If you are spending more hours than these guidelines suggest, you may be studying inefficiently; in that case, you should talk to your instructor about how to study more effectively.

If Your Course Is:	Time for Reading the Assigned Text (per week)	Time for Homework Assignments (per week)	Time for Review and Test Preparation (average per week)	Total Study Time (per week)
3 credits	2 to 4 hours	2 to 3 hours	2 hours	6 to 9 hours
4 credits	3 to 5 hours	2 to 4 hours	3 hours	8 to 12 hours
5 credits	3 to 5 hours	3 to 6 hours	4 hours	10 to 15 hours

General Strategies for Studying

- Budget your time effectively. One or two hours each day is more effective, and far less painful, than studying all night before homework is due or before exams. Note: Research shows that it can be helpful to create a "personal contract" for your study time (or for any other personal commitment), in which you specify rewards you'll give yourself for success and penalties you'll assess for failings.

- Engage your brain. Learning is an active process, not a passive experience. Whether you are reading, listening to a lecture, or working on assignments, always make sure that your mind is actively engaged. If you find your mind drifting or falling asleep, make a conscious effort to revive yourself, or take a break if necessary.

- Don't try to multitask. Research shows that human beings simply are not good at multitasking: When we attempt it, we do more poorly at all of the individual tasks. And in case you think you are an exception, the same research also shows that those people who believed they were best at multitasking were actually the worst! So when it is time to study, turn off your electronic devices, find a quiet spot, and give your work a focused effort of concentration. And if you are using a device to study (such as with an e-book or online homework), turn off e-mail, text, and other alerts so that they will not interrupt your concentration.

- Don't miss class. Listening to lectures and participating in class activities and discussions is much more effective than reading someone else's notes. Active participation will help you retain what you are learning. Also, be sure to complete any assigned reading before the class in which it will be discussed. This is crucial, since class sessions are designed to help reinforce key ideas from the reading.

- Use your textbook effectively. For a science book, for example: Begin by identifying the learning goals of an assigned chapter, and get an overview of key concepts by studying the illustrations and reading their captions. Next, read the chapter twice: On the first pass, read only the narrative, skipping any optional or boxed features; on the second pass, include the boxed features, and make notes on the pages to remind yourself of ideas you may want to review later. After you complete the reading, check your understanding by trying some of the end-of-chapter problems or any on-line quizzes or tutorials that may be available.

- Start your homework early. The more time you allow yourself, the easier it is to get help if you need it. If a concept gives you trouble, first try additional reading or studying beyond what has been assigned. If you are still having trouble, ask for help: You surely can find friends, peers, or teachers who will be glad to help you learn.

- Working together with friends can be valuable in helping you understand difficult concepts. However, be sure that you learn *with* your friends and do not become dependent on them.

Preparing for Exams

- Rework problems and other assignments; try additional questions to be sure you understand the concepts. Study your performance on assignments, quizzes, or exams from earlier in the term.

- Study your notes from classes, and reread relevant sections in your textbook. Pay attention to what your instructor expects you to know for an exam.

- Study individually *before* joining a study group with friends. Study groups are effective only if every individual comes prepared to contribute.

- Don't stay up too late before an exam. Don't eat a big meal within an hour of the exam (thinking is more difficult when blood is being diverted to the digestive system).

- Try to relax before and during the exam. If you have studied effectively, you are capable of doing well. Staying relaxed will help you think clearly.

Presenting Homework and Writing Assignments

All work that you turn in should be of *collegiate quality:* neat and easy to read, well organized, and demonstrating mastery of the subject matter. Future employers and teachers will expect this quality of work. Moreover, although submitting homework of collegiate quality requires "extra" effort, it serves two important purposes directly related to learning:

1. The effort you expend in organizing and clearly explaining your work solidifies your learning. In particular, research has shown that writing and speaking trigger different areas of your brain. By writing something down—even when you think you already understand it—you reinforce your learning by involving other areas of your brain.

2. By making your work clear and self-contained (that is, making it a document that you can read without referring to the questions in the text), you will have a much more useful study guide when you review for a quiz or exam.

The following guidelines will help ensure that your assignments meet the standards of collegiate quality:

- Always use proper grammar, proper sentence and paragraph structure, and proper spelling. Do not use texting shorthand. And don't become over-reliant on spell checkers, which may miss "too two three mistakes, to."

- All answers and other writing should be fully self-contained; that is, the question itself should be somehow "contained" in the answer. A good test is to imagine that a friend is reading your work and to ask yourself whether the friend would understand exactly what you are trying to say and why. It is also helpful to read your work out loud to yourself, making sure that it sounds clear and coherent.

- In problems that require calculation:
  - Be sure to *show your work* clearly. By doing so, both you and your instructor can follow the process you used to obtain an answer. Also, please use standard mathematical symbols, rather than "calculator-ese." For example, show multiplication with the $\times$ symbol (not with an asterisk), and write 10^5, not 10^5 or 10E5.

○ *Word problems should have word answers.* That is, after you have completed any necessary calculations, any problem stated in words should be answered with one or more *complete sentences* that describe the point of the problem and the meaning of your solution.

○ *Units are crucial.* If your answer has units, be sure they are stated clearly. For example, if you are asked to calculate a distance, be sure you state whether your answer is in miles, kilometers, or some other distance unit.

○ Express your word answers in a way that would be *meaningful* to most people. For example, most people would find it more meaningful if you express a result of 720 hours as 1 month. Similarly, if a precise calculation yields an answer of 9,745,600 years, it may be more meaningful in words as "nearly 10 million years."

- Include illustrations whenever they help explain your answer, and make sure your illustrations are neat, clear, and labeled if necessary. For example, if you graph by hand, use a ruler to make straight lines. If you use software to make illustrations, be careful not to make them overly cluttered with unnecessary features.

- If you study with friends, be sure that you turn in your own work stated in your own words — you should avoid anything that might give even the *appearance* of possible academic dishonesty.

Sample Syllabus

Many problems that tend to arise in classes can be alleviated if you are very clear about your expectations of students. Below you'll find a sample syllabus, adapted from one of my astronomy courses. If you've never taught before, you might wish to use this as a starting point for creating your own syllabus. Otherwise, it might still provide you with a few ideas of things to add or change in your current syllabus format.

Most of the sample syllabus should be self-explanatory, and the steps needed to adapt it to your own class will probably be obvious. However, here are a few brief introductory notes on some of the specific details:

- This syllabus is for a college course and will need more significant adaptation for K–12 courses.

- The specifics, such as textbook, grading, and so on, are of course only examples. You will modify to fit your own class.

- Notice three special sections that are probably useful in some form for any science class:

  ○ The "Common Courtesy Guidelines" lay out behavioral expectations; as we discussed earlier, some students are unaware of these, so it is useful to be clear about them.

  ○ The section entitled "Can I Get the Grade I Really Want?" is likely to get students' attention and helps further in putting emphasis on the fact that the key to student success is hard work.

  ○ The "Closing Promise" is designed to help students feel comfortable with what is likely to be an unfamiliar subject to them — science.

- Note that the entire schedule of assignments for the semester is laid out clearly, so that students can plan ahead. Nevertheless, a caveat is included at the top in case you decide to modify the schedule as the class progresses.

Sample Syllabus
Introductory Astronomy 1: The Solar System

Dr. Jeffrey Bennett
Tu, Th 12:30–1:45 p.m., Room 365

Office: Room 119. Phone: 303-440-9313
E-mail: jeff@bigkidscience.com;
Personal web page: www.jeffreybennett.com
Office hours/open review sessions:

- Tu, Th: 2–3 p.m., at my office.

- W, F: 12:30–1:30 p.m.—Look for me in the main dining area of the Student Union; I'll try to be at a table near the northwest corner.

- If these hours do not work for you, e-mail me to make an appointment for a time that will be convenient.

General Information

Astronomy 1 is one of two general courses in introductory astronomy. In this class we concentrate on the development of human understanding of the universe and survey current understanding of our planetary system. The other semester (Astronomy 2) explores our understanding of the structure and evolution of stars and galaxies, and current scientific theories concerning the history of the universe.

No scientific or mathematical background is assumed, beyond the entrance requirements to the university. Astronomy is a *science*, however, so you will be expected to develop your critical thinking and reasoning skills. In terms of mathematics, we will use only arithmetic and a bit of simple algebra.

Although I have taught this course many times previously, there is always room for improvement. Please feel free to offer comments, criticisms, or suggestions at any time. I will make any adjustments that are necessary to ensure that you find the course both challenging and rewarding.

Required Textbooks/Media

The textbook for this course is *The Cosmic Perspective, Seventh Edition*, by Bennett, Donahue, Schneider, and Voit. You will also need access to the MasteringAstronomy web site and a standard university clicker.

Appendices

Course Requirements and Grading

Your final grade will be based on the following work:

- Weekly Homework Assignments. Late homework will be accepted only if you have made prior arrangements and there is a very good reason for the lateness.

- Scores from Online Quizzes. You may take a quiz as many times as you wish *before* its due date, and you will be credited with your highest score. If you take a quiz late, you will be credited with the first score you get, minus a 10% late penalty.

- Class Participation. During classes, we will engage in discussions and occasional activities, some of which may involve using clickers or completing worksheets. Participation in these activities will form part of your final grade.

- Observing Sessions. We will have several nights where the campus observatory is reserved for our class. You are required to attend at least one of these observing sessions and complete the observing worksheet that will be given to you when you arrive.

- Exams. We will have two in-class midterms and one final exam. There are no make-ups. If you miss an exam due to an extenuating circumstance and can provide documentation, talk to me about the possibility of writing a paper in place of the missed exam.

Calculating Your Final Grade

Your final course grade will be weighted as follows:

Homework	25%
Quizzes	10%
Class Participation	10%
Observing Sessions	5%
Midterm 1	10%
Midterm 2	15%
Final Exam	25%
Total	100%

A final score of 99–100% will be an A+; 92–98 is an A; 90–91 is an A–; the pattern continues for each lower grade.

Common Courtesy Guidelines

For the benefit of your fellow students and your instructors, you are expected to practice common courtesy with regard to all course interactions. For example:

- Show up for class on time.
- Do not leave class early, and do not rustle papers in preparation to leave before class is dismissed.
- Be attentive in class; stay awake, don't read newspapers, and *turn off your cell phones and all other electronic devices* that might compete for your attention or distract your classmates during class time.
- If you must be late or leave early on any particular day, please inform me in advance.
- Play well with others. Be kind and respectful to your fellow students and your teachers.

You can expect your grade to be lowered if you do not practice common courtesy.

Can I Get the Grade I Really Want?

Yes—but it will depend on your effort. It does not matter whether you have ever learned anything about astronomy before or whether you are "good" in science. What does matter is your willingness to work hard. Astronomy is a demanding course, in which we will move quickly and each new topic will build on concepts covered previously. If you fall behind at any time, you will find it extremely difficult to get caught back up. If you want to get a good grade in this class, be sure to pay special attention to the following:

- Carefully read the handout (or section of your textbook Preface) called "How to Succeed in College Classes." It describes how much time you should expect to spend studying outside class and lists a number of useful suggestions about how to study efficiently.
- Don't procrastinate. The homework assignments will take you several hours each, so if you leave them to the last minute, you'll be in trouble— and it will be too late for you to ask for help. Both quizzes and homework need to be completed on time if you want to avoid late penalties.

- Don't miss class, and make sure you come to class prepared, having completed the assignments due by that date.
- Don't be a stranger to your instructor—come see me in office hours, even if you don't have any specific questions.
- If you find yourself confused or falling behind for any reason at any time, let me know immediately. No matter what is causing your difficulty, I am quite willing to work with you to find a way for you to succeed—but I can't help if I don't know there's a problem.

A Closing Promise

All the hard work described above might sound a bit intimidating, but I can make you this promise: Few topics have inspired humans throughout the ages as much as the mysteries of the heavens. This class offers you the opportunity to explore these mysteries in depth, learning both about our tremendous modern understanding of the universe and about the mysteries that remain. If you work hard and learn the material well, this class will be one of the most rewarding classes of your college career.

Schedule

The indicated assignments should be completed *before* class on the listed date.

Listen in class and check your e-mail for updates to the schedule or syllabus.

Tuesdays		Thursdays	
Aug 24	First day of class	Aug 26	Reading: Chapter 1 Online Quiz: Ch. 1
Aug 31	Reading: Chapter 2 Online Quiz: Ch. 2	Sep 2	Homework Due
Sep 7	Reading: Chapter 3 Online Quiz: Ch. 3	Sep 9	Homework Due
Sep 14	Reading: Chapter 4 Online Quiz: Ch. 4	Sep 16	Homework Due

Tuesdays		Thursdays	
Sep 21	Reading: Chapter S1 Online quiz: Ch. S1	Sep 23	Homework Due
Sep 28	Reading: Chapter 5 Online Quiz: Ch. 5	Sep 30	FIRST MIDTERM (IN CLASS)
Oct 5	Reading: Chapter 6 Online Quiz: Ch. 6	Oct 7	Homework Due
Oct 12	Reading: Chapter 7 Online Quiz: Ch. 7	Oct 14	Homework Due
Oct 19	Reading: Chapter 8 Online Quiz: Ch. 8	Oct 21	Homework Due
Oct 26	Reading: Chapter 9 Online Quiz: Ch. 9	Oct 28	Homework Due
Nov 2	Reading: Chapter 10 Online Quiz: Ch. 10	Nov 4	SECOND MIDTERM (IN CLASS)
Nov 9	Reading: Chapter 11 Online Quiz: Ch. 11	Nov 11	Homework Due
Nov 16	Reading: Chapter 12 Online Quiz: Ch. 12	Nov 18	Homework Due
Nov 23	Reading: Chapter 13 Online Quiz: Ch. 13	Nov 25	Thanksgiving Holiday—No class!
Nov 30	Reading: Chapter 24 Online Quiz: Ch. 24	Dec 2	Homework Due
Dec 7	Review		

Final Exam: Monday, Dec. 14, 3:30 p.m. – 6:30 p.m.

* Observatory nights (weather dependent): Aug. 30, Sep. 22, Oct. 6, Nov. 4, Dec. 1.

A Dwarf Quiz

3

The following dwarf quiz gets its name not only because it's short, but because it demonstrates how crazy the jargon of professional astronomers can sound to students — or even to us, once we really think about it. Obviously, it's just for fun…

1. What color is a brown dwarf?
   a. brown
   b. green
   c. magenta
   d. dwarfish

2. As a white dwarf cools over many millions of years, its color gradually changes. More technically, we say that the white dwarf changes:
   a. from a white dwarf to a red dwarf to a brown dwarf to a black dwarf
   b. from a white dwarf to a red dwarf to a black dwarf, but never becoming a brown dwarf
   c. from a white dwarf to a red dwarf to a dwarf planet
   d. directly from white dwarf to black dwarf without passing through anything else in between

3. Which dwarf can have the highest mass?
   a. Yellow dwarf
   b. Red dwarf
   c. White dwarf
   d. Brown dwarf
   e. Dwarf planet

4. Once formed, which of the following dwarfs stays its original "color" for the longest time?
   a. Yellow dwarf
   b. Orange dwarf
   c. White dwarf
   d. Brown dwarf

5. What does a yellow dwarf turn into next, after it stops being a yellow dwarf?
   a. Orange dwarf
   b. Brown dwarf
   c. White dwarf
   d. Dwarf planet
   e. Red giant

6. A "red dwarf planet" is:
   a. a dwarf planet that has a reddish color like Mars
   b. a planet orbiting a star of the most common type
   c. a dwarf planet orbiting a red giant
   d. a or b above
   e. a or c above

7. Ranking Task: Rank the following dwarfs in terms of luminosity, from greatest to smallest. (Note: If a type of dwarf comes in a range of luminosities, rank its greatest possible value.)
   A. Yellow dwarf
   B. Red dwarf
   C. White dwarf
   D. Brown dwarf
   E. Dwarf planet
   F. Dwarf galaxy

8. Ranking Task: Rank the following dwarfs in order of radius, from largest to smallest. (Note: If a type of dwarf comes in a range of radii, rank its greatest possible value.)
   A. Yellow dwarf
   B. Red dwarf
   C. White dwarf
   D. Brown dwarf
   E. Dwarf planet
   F. Dwarf galaxy

9. Although not officially defined, the term "ice dwarf" is used by many astronomers to mean a:
   a. Yellow dwarf
   b. Red dwarf
   c. White dwarf
   d. Brown dwarf
   e. Large comet

10. Astrobiology: Which of the following dwarfs is most likely to have habitable conditions either on it or on an object in orbit of it?
    a. Yellow dwarf
    b. Red dwarf
    c. White dwarf
    d. Brown dwarf
    e. Dwarf planet

11. Astrobiology: In the event of SETI success, which type of dwarf is most likely to have sent the signal to us?
    a. Red dwarf
    b. Green dwarf
    c. White dwarf
    d. Brown dwarf
    e. Dwarf planet

Answers:
1. c; 2. d; 3. c; 4. d; 5. e; 6. d; 7. F>A>B>C>D>E; 8. F>A>B>D>C>E; 9. e; 10. a; 11. This question is a joke.

Excerpts

I've included the following two book excerpts to elaborate on ideas related to teaching about the nature of science.

Excerpt 1: What Makes It Science?

The following excerpt consists of the whole of Chapter 2 from my book *Beyond UFOs: The Search for Extraterrestrial Life and Its Astonishing Implications for Our Future* (Princeton University Press, paperback edition, 2011). You can also find additional details about the nature of science in any of my astronomy and astrobiology textbooks. Reprinted with permission from Princeton University Press.

Chapter 2
What Makes It Science?

> All our science, measured against reality, is primitive and childlike—and yet it is the most precious thing we have.
> —Albert Einstein

I'd always wanted to see a real UFO—something in the sky that I could not explain and that would therefore qualify as an *unidentified* flying object. Then, even without proof, I could at least hope that I'd seen an alien spacecraft. For most of my life, it never happened. Sure, I saw lots of strange things in the sky. But with a little thought, I'd soon conclude that I'd only seen a distant airplane or a rocket trail or the planet Venus seeming to dart about as clouds passed in front of it. Ironically, I finally saw my first UFO just a few weeks after I started working on this book.

I was outside with my then 6-year-old son, Grant, watching the stars in the predawn sky. Venus was shining brightly in the east, which made me do a double take when I suddenly saw another object shining just as brightly in the west. Over the next few seconds, the object grew brighter and brighter until it was by far the brightest object in the sky. I called to Grant to look over at it. "Wow!" he said. Then, as quickly as it had brightened, it faded away. To my eyes it merely disappeared. But Grant, who as a child has much better night vision, said it darted off to the right as it vanished from view. The entire episode lasted no more than about 10 seconds.

No airplane could have moved in that way, nor could it have been a sat-ellite or rocket trail. It wasn't a planet, and it wasn't a cloud. In fact, my first thought as I watched it brighten was that I was witnessing the explosion of a distant star—a nova or a supernova. But its rapid disappearance ruled out this idea, because stellar explosions take days or weeks to fade from view. So what was it? Had I finally witnessed an alien spacecraft flying in for a quick glimpse of my town?

Possibly, but I also came up with an alternative explanation. I love my sleep almost as much as I love the stars, and we were outside at 4 AM only because it was the night of the annual Perseid meteor shower. By the time we saw the strange light, Grant and I had already seen a couple dozen meteors streaking across the sky. Could our strange light simply have been another meteor?

Meteors are created when pebble-size pieces of dust from space burn up high in our atmosphere. Particles of space dust typically plunge into the atmosphere at a speed in excess of 30,000 miles per hour. This high speed generates intense friction, making the air around the particle so hot that it glows. In other words, the flash of a meteor is the glow of hot air surround-ing a high-speed particle, rather than the particle itself. The flash ends when the particle has fully disintegrated. Most of the dust particles that crash into Earth were shed by comets that passed near Earth's orbit. We get annual meteor showers because our planet crosses the same trails of comet dust at the same time each year. The Perseid meteors get their name because the geometry of the meteor shower makes the meteors appear to emanate from the constellation Perseus as they burn up in the atmosphere.

The trouble with thinking of my light in the sky as a meteor is that it didn't act like a Perseid meteor should. It did not streak across the sky, and it did not appear to come from the direction of Perseus. In fact, because it appeared to stay nearly stationary as it brightened and faded, it could have been a meteor only if it had been coming almost straight toward us, so that it would appear motionless but brighter as it came closer. Even then, I still don't have a good explanation for the sudden movement that Grant saw at the end. Perhaps what he saw was a secondary flash as a fragment of the dust particle flew off in one direction. Or perhaps he saw an illusion created by the movement of his own head.

The bottom line is that I cannot conclusively identify the light I saw in the sky as a meteor or as anything else, which means I can truly claim to have seen an unidentified flying object. However, I cannot automatically conclude that my UFO was an alien spacecraft. It might indeed have been evidence of alien visitation, but it might also have been a rather unusual meteor. The heart of science lies in the way we choose among such competing explanations.

If I let my wishes get the best of me, I would choose the explanation of alien visitors. After all, I really want to believe that the universe is full of life and that we'll someday make contact with other civilizations. If I could just accept the idea that I experienced such contact on the night when I saw the light in the sky, then I could join the legions of people who believe with all their hearts that aliens are here among us.

But I'm either blessed or cursed with a scientific mind, and I'd therefore bet about 25 million to one that my UFO was actually an unusual meteor rather than an alien spacecraft. Why? Because every day, about 25 million pieces of space dust enter the atmosphere and burn up as meteors somewhere in Earth's sky. It seems far more reasonable to think that I saw an odd one among those 25 million rather than something as extraordinary as beings from another world. I'm reminded of a dictum from the great Carl Sagan: "Extraordinary claims require extraordinary evidence."

I tell this story not to discredit other UFO sightings but rather to emphasize what I consider to be the most basic difference between science and beliefs. Science is supposed to be based on verifiable evidence, while beliefs are matters of faith or opinion. I could believe with all my heart that I really did see an alien spacecraft, but if you don't believe me, there's nothing that either of us can do to convince the other. For an idea to be science, it has to be something that we *can* come to agreement on, at least in principle, by comparing notes on evidence that we both can study.

The idea that science is a way of helping people come to agreement may seem surprising in light of the cultural wars we often read about in the news, but it explains why science has been so successful in advancing human knowledge. Think back to the debate between Aristotle and the atomists over the question of whether there could be worlds beyond Earth. For nearly 2,000 years, this ongoing debate went essentially nowhere, because there was no way for the two sides to come to agreement on any of the issues involved. But as soon as we had solid, verifiable evidence showing that Earth is a planet going around the Sun, we knew that Aristotle's position had been wrong [because his argument was based on Earth being the center of the universe]. To be fair, while Aristotle turned out to be fundamentally incorrect in many of his beliefs about physics and astronomy, he was actually quite a good observer and made many important discoveries in other subject areas. In biology, for example, he correctly described numerous relationships between species. Where he erred, he did so because he had nothing solid to go on. If Aristotle could have returned to life in the mid-1600s and examined the overwhelming evidence demonstrating that Earth is not the center of the universe, I think he would have been quite convinced. The evidence certainly convinced the scientific community, and the agreement on this point led people to ask new questions, such as what holds Earth in its orbit as it goes around the Sun. The quest to answer these new questions ignited the scientific and technological revolution that has made our civilization what it is today.

OK, you may ask, but if science is supposed to help people come to agreement, why does it so often seem to do the opposite? Why, for example, do some religious people think that science is out to destroy their faith, and why do so many UFO believers think that science is trying to hide the truth from them? Honestly, I don't really know, but my suspicion is that those who feel threatened by science don't really understand it. If they did, they'd realize that science is indeed a tool for bringing people together with common understandings. I doubt that anyone could find fault with that, no matter what their personal views of God.

So as I step back down off my soapbox, you can probably see where we're going next. If I'm going to achieve this book's stated goal of helping you understand what science really tells us about extraterrestrial life, we need to be very clear about what science is and what it is not. Otherwise, we'll be stuck like Aristotle and the atomists in endless debate over things like my UFO in the night sky, talking and talking but never actually learning anything.

The Ancient Roots of Science

Just as we can understand a fellow human being better by knowing what she experienced in childhood, we can understand science better if we understand how it grew up. Science grew up primarily through attempts to understand the motions of the Sun, Moon, planets, and stars in the sky.

Why is it that astronomy was so important to ancient people? The first answer was practicality. In the days before mechanical and electronic devices, the only clocks and calendars were in the sky. If you wanted to know the time of day or the time of year—clearly critical information for agrarian societies—you had to know how to read them from careful observations of the Sun's position in the sky. Around the world, you can still see many amazing structures constructed largely for the purpose of telling the time or date by the Sun; famous examples include Stonehenge, Egyptian obelisks, and the Native American Sun Dagger in New Mexico. The Moon was only slightly less important. Many civilizations grew up along coastlines, so keeping track of the Moon enabled them to predict and work with the tides.

The practical importance of marking the motions of the heavens did not automatically mean that people needed to understand *why* the movements occurred. After all, you can use a watch without knowing what's going on inside of it. But just as many kids like to take watches apart to see what makes them tick, ancient people were curious about the clockwork of the sky.

Early on, in what we might call mythological times, people tended to attribute what they saw in the sky to the supernatural. If you imagined the Sun or the planets as gods, it was easy to "explain" their motions as the prerogative of those gods. Science began as people tried to move beyond the supernatural, instead trying to come up with physical mechanisms by which they could not only explain what they saw in the sky but also predict what they would see in the future. Because most ancient cultures left relatively few written records—and those few were more likely to be about politics or religion than about the search for physical explanations—we really do not know how many people in how many different cultures might have been early practitioners of science. What we do know is that this type of science was under way in Greece by about 500 B.C., and that we can trace a nearly straight line from the ancient Greek meditations to the methods of modern science.

As we discussed briefly in chapter 1, the Greeks generally assumed that Earth lay unmoving at the center of the universe, a very natural idea given that our world feels quite stationary and the sky appears to circle around us. But if they were actually going to predict the future positions of the Sun, Moon, and planets in the sky, the Greeks needed much more than just this idea. They needed a physical *model* of the universe, one that would allow them to calculate future positions with the aid of mathematics.

The first step in creating such a model is to search for patterns of motion that the model must explain. The motion of the stars was very easy: The stars stay fixed in the same constellations from night to night and year to year, and all seem simply to circle around our world once each day. Thus, to explain the motions of the stars, the Greeks envisioned a great, rotating celestial sphere surrounding our central world, with the stars arranged on the great sphere in the patterns of the constellations.

The Sun follows an only slightly more complex pattern of motion in our sky: It circles daily around us much like any star, but over the course of the year it gradually moves through the constellations along the path that we call the *ecliptic*. The Greek philosophers could explain this motion by imagining that the Sun turned around Earth on its own sphere, with the turning rate tuned so that from our viewpoint it reproduced the Sun's annual motion along the ecliptic. A third sphere took care of the Moon, which also moves steadily through the constellations, though not precisely on the same path from one month to the next.

The real difficulties for the Greek model came with the planets. Unlike the Sun and Moon, the planets do not move steadily through the constel-

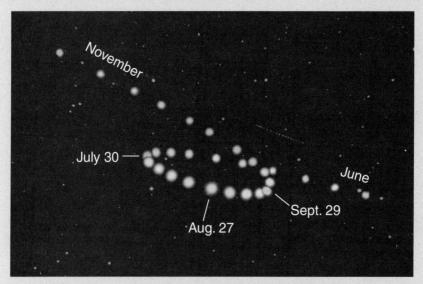

Figure 2.1. This composite of 29 photographs, each taken at five- to eight-day intervals, shows Mars between early June and late November 2003. Notice the period of "backward" motion in the middle of the loop. The white dots in a line just right of center are the planet Uranus, which by coincidence was in the same part of the sky. Photo by Tunc Tezel.

lations. The Sun moves along the ecliptic at a rate of just under 1 degree per day, which is why it takes just a few more than 360 days to circle all the way around. The Moon moves through the constellations somewhat faster—about 12 degrees per day, which is enough that you can notice this motion even on a single night by comparing the Moon's position relative to a bright star early in the evening to its position a few hours later. The planets, in contrast, seem to move among the stars in a very erratic way. Sometimes they move relatively fast from one night to the next, other times more slowly. Most strangely of all, they sometimes reverse course entirely, moving "backward" relative to the stars for a few weeks or months—a phenomenon known as *apparent retrograde motion*. For example, the composite photo in figure 2.1 shows Mars over a period of about six months; notice its retrograde loop in the middle, during which it turned around and moved "backward" compared to its normal direction of motion through the constellations.

This complex motion could not be explained just by adding another sphere for each planet, unless you were to allow the sphere's rate and direction of rotation to vary over time. But the Greeks did not allow such variations, in part because such arbitrary variations still wouldn't have offered a set of rules by which to predict future planetary positions, but more importantly because it would have violated a central tenet of Greek thought. In a doctrine enunciated most clearly by Plato (428–348 B.C.), the Greeks held that the heavens must be "perfect," which they took to mean that heavenly objects must move in "perfect" circles with perfectly constant speeds. This doctrine was so deeply ingrained in Greek thought that, as far as we know, they never seriously considered dumping it, no matter how much it seemed to disagree with observations. And why did they hold this doctrine so dear? We really don't know; they just did. It certainly wasn't backed by any actual evidence. It was just something they believed.

In any event, faced with the reality that the planets sometimes move backward relative to the stars, the Greeks faced essentially two choices for how they could go about trying to explain this phenomenon. Behind Door #1 (so to speak) lay the choice that we now know to be the truth: The planets don't really ever go backward, they just seem to as we pass by them in our orbit of the Sun. You can see how this works with the simple demonstration shown in figure 2.2. Have a friend walk in a circle to represent Mars's orbit while you walk in a circle to represent Earth's orbit; be sure you walk faster than your friend, since inner planets orbit the Sun faster than outer planets. If you watch your friend's position against objects in the back-

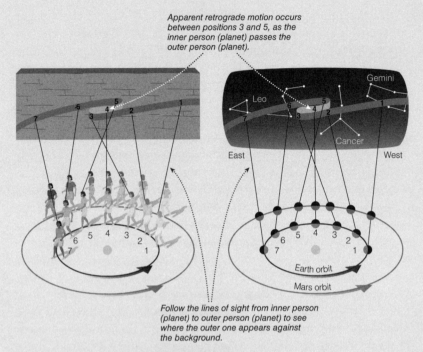

Figure 2.2. The real explanation for the fact that planets sometimes move "backward" relative to the stars: The demonstration on the left shows the basic idea, and the diagram on the right shows how it applies to Mars.

ground, you'll see that your friend *seems* to go backward as you "lap" her in your orbit, even though she never really reverses course. As the second illustration shows, the same idea explains why we see the real Mars sometimes move backward relative to the stars. Alternatively, the Greeks could choose the explanation behind Door #2, in which they could hold to their notion of spheres surrounding Earth by attempting to come up with an extraordinarily convoluted and complex model of spheres turning inside of other spheres, with each sphere in some different rotational orientation, with the ultimate hope of making the whole combination lead to something that would predict planetary positions at least moderately well.

With our modern-day hindsight, it might seem strange to think that anyone would choose Door #2 over Door #1, but with a few notable exceptions—such as Aristarchus, whom we encountered in chapter 1—that's exactly what the Greeks did. Why did they choose a complex and convoluted explanation when a far simpler one was available? In part, it's because the correct answer would have forced them to throw out the idea of Earth as the center of the universe, and many of them probably thought that to be a far too radical solution. However, many Greek philosophers apparently gave serious consideration to Aristarchus's suggestion, and actually rejected it on its merits as they were understood at the time.

In particular, Aristarchus's idea [that Earth orbits the Sun] seemed inconsistent with observations of stellar positions in the sky. To understand why, imagine what would happen if you placed the Sun rather than Earth at the center of the celestial sphere, with Earth orbiting the Sun some distance away. In that case, Earth would be closer to different portions of the celestial sphere at different times of year. When we were closer to a particular part of the sphere, the stars on that part of the sphere would appear more widely separated than they would when we were farther from that part of the sphere, just as the spacing between the two headlights on a car looks greater when you are closer to the car. This would create annual shifts in the separations of stars—but the Greeks observed no such shifts. They knew that there were only two possible ways to account for the lack of an observed shift: Either Earth was at the center of the universe, or the stars were so far away as to make the shift undetectable by eye. To most Greeks, it seemed unreasonable to imagine that the stars could be *that* far away, which therefore left them with the conclusion that Earth must hold a central place.

Significantly, this basic argument still holds when we allow for the reality that stars lie at different distances rather than all on the same sphere. As Earth orbits the Sun, we look at the stars from different positions in space at different times of year. Just as your finger will seem to shift back and forth against the background if you hold it at arm's length and alternately blink your left and right eyes, nearby stars should seem to shift against the background of more distant stars as we look at them at different times of year from opposite sides of Earth's orbit. Although such shifts (called *stellar parallax*) are much too small to measure with the naked eye, they are easily detectable with modern telescopes and therefore represent concrete proof that Earth really does go around the Sun. In fact, precise measurement of these shifts provides us a direct way to measure the distances to stars; the method is essentially the same method of "triangulation" that construction workers use to measure distances here on the ground.

Unable to detect these stellar shifts and therefore having concluded that Earth must really be in the center of things, for several centuries the Greeks developed new and ever-more-complex ways of getting their Earth-centered model to make predictions that agreed with reality. This long effort culminated with the work of the Greek astronomer Ptolemy (pronounced *TOL-e-mee*; c. A.D. 100–170), who published a detailed and mathematically precise treatise that could be used to predict the future positions of planets among the stars. The required calculations were both very complex and extraordinarily tedious; many centuries later, while supervising calculations based on the Ptolemaic model, the Spanish monarch Alphonso X (1221–1284) is said to have complained that "If I had been present at the creation, I would have recommended a simpler design for the universe." Nevertheless, Ptolemy's model worked remarkably well, as it generally allowed planetary positions to be predicted to an accuracy of a few degrees—roughly equivalent to the size of your hand viewed at arm's length against the sky. This was an astonishing achievement at the time, and may be even more impressive with modern hindsight, since we now know that Ptolemy got these good answers even though he started from the fundamentally wrong idea that Earth is the center of the universe. When Arabic scholars translated Ptolemy's book describing the model, around A.D. 800, they gave it the title *Almagest*, derived from words meaning "the greatest compilation."

The great success of Ptolemy's model represented both the best and the worst of ancient Greek science. On the positive side, the model gained acceptance because it made predictions that agreed reasonably well with reality, and insistence on such agreement remains at the heart of modern science today. On the negative side, the model was so convoluted that it's unlikely that anyone, including Ptolemy himself, thought that it actually represented the true nature of the cosmos. Indeed, the model was not even fully self-consistent, as different mathematical tricks needed to be used to calculate the positions of different planets. Today, these negatives would weigh so heavily against any scientific idea that people would go immediately back to the drawing board in search of something that worked better. But in Ptolemy's time, these negatives were apparently acceptable, and it was another 1,500 years before they were revisited.

The Copernican Revolution

The Greek ideas gained great influence in the ancient world, in large part because the Greeks proved to be as adept at politics and war as they were at philosophy. In about 330 B.C., Alexander the Great began a series of conquests that expanded the Greek Empire throughout the Middle East. Alexander was deeply interested in science and education, perhaps because he grew up with Aristotle as his personal tutor. Alexander established the city of Alexandria in Egypt, which soon became home to the greatest library the world had ever seen. The Library of Alexandria remained the world's pre-eminent center of research for some 700 years. At its peak, it may have held more than a half million books, all handwritten on papyrus scrolls. When the library was finally destroyed during a time of anti-intellectual fervor in the fifth century A.D., most of the ancient Greek writings were lost forever.

Much more would have been lost if not for the rise of a new center of intellectual achievement in Baghdad (in present-day Iraq). While European civilization fell into the Dark Ages, scholars of the new religion of Islam sought knowledge of mathematics and astronomy in hopes of better understanding the wisdom of Allah. The Islamic scholars—often working collaboratively with Christians and Jews—translated and thereby saved many of the remaining ancient Greek works. Building on what they learned from the Greek manuscripts, they went on to develop the mathematics of algebra as well as many new instruments and techniques for astronomical observation.

The Islamic world of the Middle Ages was in frequent contact with Hindu scholars from India, who in turn brought ideas and discoveries from China. Hence, the intellectual center in Baghdad achieved a synthesis of the surviving work of the ancient Greeks, the Indians, the Chinese, and the con-tributions of its own scholars. This accumulated knowledge spread through-out the Byzantine Empire (the eastern part of the former Roman Empire). When the Byzantine capital of Constantinople (modern-day Istanbul) fell in 1453, many Eastern scholars headed west to Europe, carrying with them the knowledge that helped ignite the European Renaissance.

The Renaissance brought a new spirit of inquiry, and technology helped fuel its spread. The most significant new technology was the printing press with movable type, invented by Johannes Gutenberg around 1450. Prior to its invention, books had to be laboriously copied by hand or printed from hand-carved pages of type. Indeed, books were so expensive and rare that few people had access to them, which is probably a major reason why most people of the time remained illiterate. The printing press changed all that. By 1500, some 9 million printed copies of some 30,000 works were in circu-lation. With books cheap and widely available, many more people learned to read. This had the effect of democratizing knowledge and naturally led to a much larger pool of scholars. The stage was set for a dramatic rethink-ing of our place in the universe, and of the principles of science as a means for advancing knowledge. The revolution began with Nicholas Copernicus (1473–1543).

The dramatic story of the Copernican revolution has been recounted many times; if you are interested in details, I encourage you to read (or watch) Carl Sagan's *Cosmos*, which is where I first learned of many of these details myself. Here, I want to focus only on how the Copernican revolution helped shape the nature of modern science.

Copernicus has his name attached to the revolution because he started people thinking about whether they should switch to his new Sun-centered model or stick with Ptolemy's old Earth-centered model. However, while his new model generated intense interest in the scholarly community, it actually won very few converts in the decades after its publication, and this failure came about for a very good reason: Despite having put Earth in its correct place, Copernicus's model did no better than Ptolemy's at predicting planetary positions.

Why didn't it work better? Blame it on Plato. In removing Earth from its central position, Copernicus willingly overthrew thousands of years of tradition and suggested an idea that would radically alter our view of our place in the universe. But he was not willing to overturn Plato's ancient dictum that heavenly motion must be in perfect circles. Because planets do *not* really orbit the Sun in perfect circles, Copernicus could not get his model to work any better than Ptolemy's, even when he added his own set of rather unrealistic orbital complexities.

Still, with things like its much more natural explanation for retrograde motion of the planets, the Sun-centered model offered an aesthetic attraction that many other scientists could not resist. Instead of ignoring Copernicus, they sought ways to make his model work better. The key players in this effort were Tycho Brahe (1546–1601) and his one-time apprentice, Johannes Kepler (1571–1630). Tycho, recognizing the importance of quality data against which any model could be checked, spent some three decades carefully recording what were by far the most accurate observations of planetary positions that had ever been made. Working before the invention of the telescope, he built large, naked-eye observatories that worked much like giant protractors, and he used them to measure planetary positions in the sky accurate to within 1 minute of arc—equivalent to less than the thickness of a fingernail held at arm's length. Kepler inherited these data after Tycho's death in 1601, and then set about trying to come up with a model of planetary motion that could match Tycho's observations.

Copernicus was a revolutionary, Tycho collected the key data, and later figures like Galileo and Newton did the work that sealed the case for the Copernican revolution. But for my money, it is Kepler to whom we most owe the birth of modern civilization, because he did something that no one else had been willing to do in the preceding 2,000 years: He trusted the data more than he trusted his own deeply held beliefs.

Kepler was a devout Christian and believed that understanding the geometry of the heavens would bring him closer to God. Like Copernicus, he believed in Plato's dictum about circular motion in the heavens, so he worked diligently to match circular orbits to Tycho's data. After years of effort, he found a set of circular orbits that matched Tycho's observations quite well. Even in the worst cases, which were for the planet Mars, Kepler's predicted positions differed from Tycho's observations by only about 8 arc-minutes—meaning that his model predicted a position that differed from Tycho's written position by an amount barely one-fourth the angular size of the full moon. Ask yourself: What would you have done in Kepler's place, having spent years developing a model that was *that close* to perfection? Would you have said, "Well, Tycho must have made a mistake when he recorded those few observations that don't match my work"? Or would you have trusted the data, thrown out your years of effort, chucked your deep belief in perfect circles, and started all over again? It gives me goose bumps every time I really think about the fact that Kepler chose option 2. About this choice, it is worth reading the words of Kepler himself:

> If I had believed that we could ignore these eight minutes [of arc], I would have patched up my hypothesis accordingly. But, since it was not permissible to ignore, those eight minutes pointed the road to a complete reformation in astronomy.

Kepler abandoned perfect circles and began testing other orbital shapes. It again took him some years of work, but he finally hit upon the correct answer: Planetary orbits are not circles, but rather are the special types of ovals known as *ellipses*. Using his talents at mathematics, he worked out the mathematical details of the elliptical orbits, which we now describe as *Kepler's laws of planetary motion*. With these laws, anyone could predict the past, present, or future positions of any of the planets known at the time. Kepler's model not only produced a perfect match to Tycho's data, but its predictions of future planetary positions were also a perfect match to what was eventually observed. I'm no historian myself, but as I understand it from Harvard historian Owen Gingerich, one of the most crucial events occurred in 1631, a couple of decades after Kepler published his model. During that year, astronomers observed a relatively rare event called a *transit* of Mercury, when Mercury appears to pass directly across the face of the Sun. The transit occurred precisely as Kepler's laws predicted it would.

Neither Ptolemy's model nor Copernicus's model nor any other model that anyone came up with could claim the same success.

It's important to realize that the failure of other models did not necessarily mean that Kepler's model was right, and even the great success of Kepler's laws did not *prove* they are true. Indeed, while there are many cases in the history of science where a model has been proven wrong, it is virtually impossible to prove a model right. The reason is that no matter how many successes a model may have, you can never be absolutely certain that it will still work in new cases. If, after Kepler's work, astronomers had discovered a new planet that did not obey Kepler's laws, they would have been forced to conclude that Kepler's laws did not always work and therefore would have either modified them or dumped them in favor of something else. That's just the way science works.

In fact, Kepler's laws are *not* perfect. Applied strictly, we know of many cases in which planets deviate from them in small but measurable ways. So why do we still accept that Kepler was right about planets orbiting the Sun along elliptical paths? The answer to this question is a key to understanding the difference between science today and science in ancient times, and hence to understanding why human knowledge is now advancing so rapidly: Back in ancient times, once a model (such as Ptolemy's) worked "good enough," people basically left it at that. But in modern science, we turn every answer into the next question.

From the moment that Kepler published his laws of planetary motion, other scientists asked questions about them. Some questioned whether they were consistent with other physical laws, since the idea of a moving Earth violated Aristotle's still-popular claims of natural motion. It took Galileo's work to prove that Aristotle had been wrong about physics, too, and thereby to seal the triumph of the Copernican idea. (Galileo's telescopic observations also played a major role, since these observations were consistent with Earth going around the Sun but could not be explained by the geocentric model.) Other scientists asked *why* Kepler's laws worked so well; after all, there was no known reason why orbits should be ellipses rather than circles or even squares. Scientists wrestled with this question for nearly 70 years before Sir Isaac Newton (1642–1727) came up with an answer. And in finding this answer, Newton not only discovered the more general laws of motion and the law of gravity, but he also had to invent the mathematics of calculus in order to prove that these new laws did indeed explain Kepler's laws.

Newton's laws did not stop the questioning either, even after they proved so successful that later scientists used them to *predict* the existence of the planet Neptune before it was actually discovered through a telescope. Message to those who believe their horoscopes: Astrology claims to be able to predict the future based on planetary positions among the stars; and yet, for thousands of years, no astrologers ever realized that they were missing an undiscovered planet that is more than a dozen times as large as Earth. Astronomy found it, astrology didn't. That doesn't necessarily prove that astronomy will always be right, but it sure looks bad for the competition.

So while the astrologers just added Neptune to their horoscopes and went on like nothing else had changed, the astronomers kept questioning. And, by the late 1800s, they had indeed found something that didn't perfectly match the predictions of Newton's law of gravity. It was Mercury's orbit that wasn't quite obeying Newton, and it forced scientists to think again about what might be going on. The eventual result was Einstein's general theory of relativity, which gives essentially the same answers as Newton's theory for planets farther from the Sun, but a slightly different answer for close-in Mercury—an answer that matches the observations. In other words, at its core, Einstein's theory is a description of gravity, and it is the best description of gravity that we have because it works in every case that Newton's description worked and more. But scientists keep questioning, and today we know that even Einstein's theory cannot be the entire story, because it fails to explain what happens to gravity on the smallest, subatomic scales.

The quest to find an improvement on Einstein is one of the driving forces in physics today. Scientists have a lot of ideas about what this improvement might look like but, so far, no actual evidence with which to choose among the competing ideas. As a result, today we are in a position of knowing that a deeper understanding of gravity must be out there, but not knowing what it actually is. This type of unanswered question is what makes science so exciting, and it drives home the point I began with, that science is a way of helping people come to agreement. Today, many different scientists have many different ideas about what the new theory of gravity should be, but ultimately, when the evidence comes in, we'll be able to choose among the competing ideas and come to agreement about which ones must go and which ones are worth taking forward into the future.

Hallmarks of Modern Science

We've discussed how the Copernican revolution gave rise to modern science, but we still haven't said exactly what science is. Indeed, you may have noticed that I've described science in several different ways already. In chapter 1, I said that science is a way of distinguishing possibilities from realities. In this chapter, I've said that science is a way of choosing among alternate explanations, and of getting people to agree. All these things are true, but they don't give us a clear way of deciding what qualifies as science and what does not. For that, we need a clearer definition of science.

Defining science is a surprisingly tall order. The word itself comes from the Latin *scientia,* meaning "knowledge," but not all knowledge is science. For example, you may know what music you like best, but your musical taste is not a result of scientific study. So what exactly is it that makes something science?

Scientists, historians, and philosophers have written hundreds of books and articles attempting to come up with a clear definition of science. Not everyone agrees on all the key points, which we can take as an illustration of the fact that semantics is not itself a science, since it does not offer us a clear way to come to agreement. Nevertheless, if you sift through all the history from the Greeks to the Copernican revolution and beyond, I believe that you'll find that everything that qualifies as science shares the following three characteristics, which I will refer to as the three hallmarks of science:

- Modern science seeks explanations for observed phenomena that rely solely on natural causes.
- Science progresses through the creation and testing of models of nature that explain the observations as simply as possible.
- A scientific model must make testable predictions about natural phenomena that would force us to revise or abandon the model if the predictions do not agree with observations.

We can see each of these hallmarks in the story of the Copernican revolution. The first shows up in the way Tycho's careful observations of planetary motion motivated Kepler to come up with a better explanation for those motions. The second is evident in the way several competing models were compared and tested, most notably those of Ptolemy, Copernicus, and Kepler. We see the third in the fact that each model could make precise predictions about the future motions of the Sun, Moon, planets, and stars in our sky. Kepler's model gained acceptance because it worked, while the competing models lost favor because their predictions failed to match the observations.

These three hallmarks are so important that it's worth considering each of them in a little more detail. Let's start with the first, which happens to lie at the root of the current debate about whether "intelligent design" should be taught in science classes. Proponents of intelligent design claim that life is so intricate and complex that it could not have arisen naturally, and they therefore claim that life must have been deliberately designed by an intelligent Designer. Personally, I find their evidence of design far less than compelling, but that's really beside the point. The real question is whether their idea should qualify as a competing scientific model that could then be taught as an alternative to the theory of evolution. If you accept the usual definition of science, then intelligent design clearly does not qualify, because it violates the first hallmark: Rather than seeking natural causes for life, intelligent design posits that life is the work of a supernatural Designer* who is beyond our scientific comprehension. That is why those who want to teach "ID" in science classes (such as the Kansas Board of Education in 2005) have attempted to redefine science so that it does not have to be solely about natural causes.

The trouble with these attempts to redefine the first hallmark is that they would render science pointless. As a simple analogy, consider the collapse of a bridge. If you choose to believe that the collapse was an act of God, you might well be right—but this belief won't help you design a better bridge. We learn to build better bridges only by assuming that collapses happen through natural causes that we can understand and learn from. In precisely the same way, it is the scientific quest for a natural understanding of life that has led to the discovery of relationships between species, genetics, DNA, and virtually all modern medicine. Many of the scientists who made these discoveries, including Charles Darwin himself, believed deeply that they could see God's hand in creation. But if they had let their belief stop them from seeking natural explanations, they would have discovered nothing. Intelligent design may or may not be true, and it may be worth discussing in philosophy classes. But if we allow science to be redefined to accommo-

---

* When a similar discussion in a sidebar in my astronomy textbook drew complaints from a few ID proponents, I learned that some of them claim that the Designer need not be supernatural. But this is just semantics: If you believe that you've found evidence that life could not have evolved through the natural mechanisms of evolution, then by defi-nition you are saying that a non-natural process intervened. To me, supernatural and non-natural are synonymous, but if you disagree, just substitute "a process that cannot be explained by Darwin's theory of evolution by natural selection." The meaning of my sentence won't change.

date it, we will undermine everything that makes science so successful in advancing human knowledge.

Let's turn next to the second hallmark, where it is the criterion of simplicity that is most often misunderstood. To see why this idea is so important, you need only to remember that Copernicus's original model did *not* match the data noticeably better than Ptolemy's model. If scientists had judged Copernicus's model solely on the accuracy of its predictions, they might have rejected it immediately. However, many scientists found elements of the Copernican model appealing, such as the simplicity of its explanation for apparent retrograde motion. They therefore kept the model alive until Kepler found a way to make it work.

In fact, if agreement with data were the sole criterion for judgment, we could imagine a modern-day Ptolemy adding millions or billions of additional complexities to his Earth-centered model in an effort to improve its agreement with observations. In principle, a sufficiently complex model could reproduce the observations with almost perfect accuracy—but according to the way we view science today, the model still would not convince us that Earth is the center of the universe. We would still choose the Copernican view over the geocentric view because its predictions would be just as accurate yet would follow from a much simpler model of nature. The idea that we should prefer the simpler of two models that agree equally well with observations is often called *Occam's razor*, after the medieval scholar William of Occam (1285–1349). Like the idea that science should seek natural rather than supernatural causes, it is not any sort of absolute rule, but rather a guideline that has proven its value in the cause of scientific progress.

The third hallmark of science begs the question of what counts as an "observation" against which a prediction can be tested. To take us back to the main topic of this book, consider the claim that aliens are visiting Earth in UFOs. Proponents of this claim say that the many thousands of eyewitness observations of UFO encounters provide evidence that it is true. But should these personal testimonials count as *scientific* evidence? On the surface, the answer may not be obvious, because all scientific studies involve eyewitness accounts on some level. For example, relatively few scientists have personally made detailed tests of Einstein's theory of relativity, and it is their personal reports of the results that have convinced other scientists of the theory's validity. However, there's a very important difference between personal testimony about a scientific test and an observation of a UFO: The first is at least in principle verifiable by anyone, while the second is not.

Understanding this difference is crucial to understanding what counts as science and what does not. Even though you may never have conducted a test of Einstein's theory of relativity yourself, there's nothing stopping you from doing so. It might require several years of study before you have the necessary background to conduct the test, but you could then confirm the results reported by other scientists. In other words, while you may currently be trusting the eyewitness testimony of scientists, you always have the option of verifying their testimony for yourself.

In contrast, there is no way for you to verify someone's eyewitness account of a UFO. Without hard evidence such as photographs or pieces of the UFO, there is nothing that you could evaluate for yourself, even in principle. (In the next chapter I'll discuss those cases where "hard evidence" for UFO sightings *has* been presented.) Moreover, scientific studies of eyewitness testimony show it to be notoriously unreliable. For example, different eyewitnesses often disagree on what they saw even immediately after an event has occurred; my own story at the beginning of this chapter is a case in point, since Grant and I have different versions of what happened to the flash of light as it disappeared from view. As time passes, memories of the event may change further. In some cases in which memory has been checked against reality, people have reported vivid memories of events that never happened at all. This explains something that virtually all of us have experienced: disagreements with a friend about who did what and when. Since both people cannot be right in such cases, at least one person must have a memory that differs from reality.

The demonstrated unreliability of eyewitness testimony explains why it is generally considered insufficient for a conviction in criminal court; at least some other evidence, such as motive, is required. And it is for the same reason that we cannot accept eyewitness testimony by itself as evidence in science, no matter who reports it or how many people offer similar testimony.

Beyond UFOs

My personal UFO remains unidentified, leaving me free to believe what I want of it. If I want to, I can decide to follow my heart and imagine that I caught a glimpse of some of the intelligent beings who I really do believe share our universe with us. Or, I can keep my usual skepticism, and hold fast to my argument that it was more likely just a meteor.

And now I think you can understand the title of this book. No matter what I may believe about my UFO, there is nothing I can do to convince you that my belief is correct, especially if you are as skeptical as me. Some people think that makes skepticism bad, but I don't. It just means that instead of trying to convince you that aliens exist by telling you what I saw with my eyes, I need to go about it by concentrating on evidence that we can examine together. And that means we need to go beyond UFOs, and beyond arguments based solely on personal beliefs and opinions, and turn to science. Only through science will we actually learn something about other life in the universe, if indeed it exists.

Excerpt 2: Evolution in the Classroom

The following excerpt consists of two subsections from Chapter 4 of my book *Beyond UFOs: The Search for Extraterrestrial Life and Its Astonishing Implications for Our Future* (Princeton University Press, paperback edition, 2011). Reprinted with permission from Princeton University Press.

Understanding Evolution

Evolution is probably the single most misunderstood idea in all of science, which probably explains why so many people do battle over it. After all, it's a lot easier to argue with something by drawing caricatures of it than by actually digging in to understand it. But like most of the great, unifying principles of science, the theory of evolution has an underlying simplicity that anyone can appreciate with just a little bit of effort. Because evolution is so important to defining life, and hence to the search for life in the universe, I hope you won't mind if I spend a few pages in an attempt to demystify it.

The word *evolution* simply means "change with time," and the idea that life might evolve through time goes back more than 2,500 years. The Greek scientist Anaximander (c. 610–547 B.C.) promoted the idea that life originally arose in water and gradually evolved from simpler to more complex forms. A century later, Empedocles (c. 492–432 B.C.) suggested that creatures poorly adapted to their environments would perish, foreshadowing the modern idea of evolutionary adaptation. Many of the early Greek atomists probably held similar beliefs, though the evidence is sparse. Aristotle, however, maintained that species are fixed and independent of one another and do not evolve. This Aristotelian view eventually became entrenched within the theology of Christianity, with the result that evolution was not taken seriously again for some 2,000 years.

By the mid-1700s, scientists were beginning to recognize that many fossils represented extinct ancestors of living species, and the idea that Earth was quite old was gaining widespread acceptance. However, no one yet knew *how* species might change with time. For that, we needed a model that could describe the mechanism of evolutionary change.

The first serious model for evolution was proposed in the early 1800s by the French naturalist Jean Baptiste Lamarck. He proposed a mechanism known as "inheritance of acquired characteristics," in which he suggested that organisms develop new characteristics during their lives and then pass these characteristics on to their offspring. For example, Lamarck would have imagined that weightlifting would enable a person to create an adaptation of great strength that could be genetically passed to his or her children. While this hypothesis may have seemed quite reasonable at the time, it has not stood up to scientific scrutiny and, following the scientific practices I outlined in chapter 2, it has therefore been discarded as a model of how evolution occurs. It has been replaced by a different model, proposed by the British naturalist Charles Darwin.

Charles Darwin described his theory of evolution in his book *The Origin of Species*, first published in 1859. In this book, Darwin laid out the case for evolution in two fundamental ways. First, he described his observations of living organisms, made during his five-year voyage on the HMS *Beagle*, and showed how they supported the idea that evolutionary change really does occur. Second, he put forth a new model of how evolution occurs, backing up his model with a wealth of evidence. In essence, the fossil record and the observed relationships between species together provide strong evidence that evolution *has* occurred, while Darwin's theory of evolution explains *how* it occurs.

You can find descriptions of Darwin's theory in almost any biology text (at least at the college level; sadly, political pressures have caused it often to be watered down for the high school level), but its basic logic was described with particular elegance by biologist Stephen Jay Gould (1941–2002). As Gould put it, Darwin built his model from "two undeniable facts and an inescapable conclusion":

Fact 1: Overproduction and competition for survival. Any localized population of a species has the potential to produce far more offspring than the local environment can support with resources such as food and shelter. This overproduction leads to a competition for survival among the individuals of the population.

Fact 2: Individual variation. Individuals in a population of any species vary in many heritable traits (traits passed from parents to offspring). No two individuals are exactly alike, and some individuals possess traits that make them better able to compete for food and other vital resources.

Inescapable conclusion: Unequal reproductive success. In the struggle for survival, those individuals whose traits best enable them to survive and reproduce will, on average, leave the largest number of offspring that in turn survive to reproduce. Therefore, in any local environment, heritable traits that enhance survival and successful reproduction will become progressively more common in succeeding generations.

It is this unequal reproductive success that Darwin called *natural selection*: Over time, advantageous genetic traits will naturally win out (be "selected") over less advantageous traits because they are more likely to be passed down through many generations. This process explains how species can change in response to their environment—by favoring traits that improve adaptation—and thus is the primary mechanism of evolution. That is, life evolves as natural selection leads over time to evolutionary adaptations that make species better suited to their environments. When the adaptations are significant enough, organisms carrying the adaptations may be so different from their ancestors that they constitute an entirely new species.

Darwin backed his logical claim that evolution proceeds through natural selection by carefully documenting a prodigious amount of evidence. His most famous evidence came from his studies of the unique species of the Galápagos Islands. For example, the islands have 13 distinct finch species ("Darwin's finches"), with different species on different islands and each species adapted to survive in its own peculiar way. Darwin recognized that this made perfect sense when considered in the context of natural selection: Some time in the past, an ancestral pair of finches reached the Galápagos from the mainland (perhaps by being blown off course by winds). Over time, local populations of island finches gradually adapted to different environments, ultimately becoming the distinct species that he observed.

Darwin recognized similar patterns among many other species in the Galápagos and elsewhere in his round-the-world voyage on the HMS *Beagle*, as well as in patterns he saw when comparing fossils of extinct organisms to modern species found in the same regions. He also found strong support for his theory of evolution by looking at examples of *artificial selection*—the selective breeding of domesticated plants or animals by humans. Dogs offer a powerful example: Breeds as different as Rottweilers and Chihuahuas were bred from a common ancestor within just a few thousand years. Darwin recognized that if artificial selection could cause such profound changes in just thousands of years, natural selection could do far more over the millions or billions of years during which it has operated.

Today, we can observe natural selection occurring right before our eyes. In many places on Earth, species have changed in time spans as short as a few decades in response to human-induced environmental changes. On a microbial level, natural selection is what allows a population of bacteria to become resistant to specific antibiotics; those few bacteria that acquire a genetic trait of resistance are the only ones that survive in the presence of the antibiotic. Indeed, bacterial cases of natural selection pose a difficult problem for modern medicine, because bacteria can quickly develop resistance to almost any new drug we produce. As a result, pharmaceutical companies are constantly working to develop new antibiotics as bacteria become resistant to existing ones. Viruses can evolve even faster, which is one reason it has proven so difficult to fight viral diseases such as the common cold, influenza, and AIDS.

All of this observational evidence makes an incredibly strong case for the theory of evolution, but in the past few decades the case has grown far stronger still. Not only do we now observe the results of evolution, but thanks to our modern understanding of DNA, we can explain exactly what takes place on a molecular level. The molecular basis of evolution comes directly from the same imperfect copying of DNA that enables individual variation.

DNA replication proceeds with remarkable speed and accuracy. Some bacteria can copy their complete genomes in a matter of minutes, and copying the complete 3-billion-base sequence in human DNA takes a human cell only a few hours. In terms of accuracy, the copying process generally occurs with less than one error *per billion* bases copied. Nevertheless, errors (mutations) do sometimes occur. For example, the wrong base may occasionally get attached in a base pair, as in the case of linking C to A rather than to G. In other cases, an extra base may be accidentally inserted into a gene, a base may be deleted, or an entire sequence of bases might be duplicated or eliminated. Absorption of ultraviolet light or nuclear radiation or the action of certain chemicals (carcinogens) can also cause mutations to occur in DNA, and once these changes are made they can be copied when the DNA gets copied.

When a daughter cell inherits a mutated DNA molecule, the mutation can affect the functionality of the cell. Many mutations are lethal, in which case the daughter cell does not live to reproduce. However, if the cell survives, the mutation will be copied every time the DNA is replicated. In that case, the mutation represents a permanent change in the cell's hereditary information. If the cell happens to be one that gets passed to the organism's offspring—as is always the case for single-celled organisms and can be the case for animals if the mutation occurs in an egg or sperm cell—the offspring will have a gene that differs from that of the parent. It is this process of mutation, along with the shuffling of genes in sexual reproduction, that leads to variation among individuals in a species (Fact #2 above). Each of us differs slightly from all other humans because we each possess a unique genome with slightly different base sequences.

Mutations therefore provide the molecular basis for evolution.* Given that different individuals of a species possess slightly different genes, it is inevitable that some genes will provide advantageous adaptations to the environment. As outlined above, the combination of individual variation and population pressure leads to natural selection, in which the advantageous adaptations are preferentially passed down through the generations. Thus, what was once a random mutation in a single individual can eventually become the "normal" version of the gene for an entire species, thereby explaining how species evolve through time.

Our detailed understanding of how evolution proceeds on a molecular level, coupled with all the other evidence for evolution collected by Darwin and others, puts the theory of evolution by natural selection on a solid foundation. In other words, it is a true *scientific theory*, by which we mean a model that has been carefully checked and tested and that has passed every test yet presented to it. Like any scientific theory, the theory of evolution can never be proven beyond all doubt. But to say it is "only a theory" reveals only ignorance of what it is all about.

Evolution in the Classroom

We have covered enough to understand the importance of evolution and how it helps shape our definition of life, which means we should be ready to move on and discuss the implications of these ideas to the search for life on other worlds. But by this point in the book, you probably know I can't step off my soapbox quite so quickly when I'm on a roll, and this topic is way too important to the future of our nation to let it go quite yet. I'm not kidding; you've seen the studies about how America is falling behind in math and science education, and the poor state of education about evolution is a key reason why. After all, if we can't teach our children about the most impor-

---

* Evolution sometimes occurs in an even more dramatic way: In some cases, organisms can transfer entire genes to other organisms, a process called *lateral gene transfer*. This process is one of the primary ways that bacteria gain resistance to antibiotics. We humans have also learned to use this process for our benefit through what we call *genetic engineering*, in which we take a gene from one organism and insert it into another. For example, genetic engineering has allowed us to produce human insulin for diabetic patients: The human gene for insulin is inserted into bacteria, and these bacteria produce insulin that can be extracted and used as medicine. Lateral gene transfer can change a species more rapidly than individual mutations, but mutations are still the underlying basis, since they created the genes in the first place.

tant and unifying discovery in the history of biology, how can we expect them to learn science at all?

When the opponents of teaching evolution offer their "only a theory" stickers, they are trying to make a distinction between "facts" and "theories." There are some cases in which such a distinction is valid, but in this case it is a false choice, analogous to asking whether gravity is fact or a theory. Gravity is a *fact* in that objects really do fall down and planets really do orbit the Sun, but we use the *theory* of gravity to explain exactly how and why these things occur. The theory of gravity is not presumed to be perfect and indeed has at least one known flaw (its inconsistency with quantum mechanics on very small scales). Moreover, Newton's original theory of gravity is now considered only an approximation to Einstein's improved theory of gravity, which itself will presumably be found to be an approximation to a more complete theory that has not yet been discovered.

The same idea holds for evolution. Nearly all scientists consider evolution to be a fact, because both the fossil record and observations of modern species make clear that living organisms really do change with time. We use the *theory* of evolution to explain how and why these changes occur. The theory of evolution clearly explains the major features of life on Earth, but as with the theory of gravity, scientists still debate the details. For example, there is considerable debate about the rate at which evolution proceeds: Some scientists suspect that evolution is "punctuated," with periods of rapid change followed by long periods in which species remain quite stable, while others suspect that evolution proceeds at a steadier pace. This debate can be quite heated between individual scientists, but it does not change the overall idea that life evolves, and it is a debate that will eventually be settled by evidence. Indeed, we can draw a direct analogy between Darwin's original theory of evolution by natural selection and Newton's original theory of gravity: Just as Newton's theory captured the main features of gravity but has been refined and improved over time, Darwin's theory captured the main features of evolution and has been refined and improved as we've gained a deeper understanding of DNA and relationships among species. And like the theory of gravity, the theory of evolution remains a work in progress. Perhaps someday we'll be able to broaden the theory through the study of comparative evolution, in which we'll explore the similarities and differences among living organisms on multiple worlds. But it is highly unlikely that we'll ever find any fundamental flaw in the basic theory of evolution by natural selection.

Another incorrect claim often made by opponents of teaching evolution is that evolution is not really science. To understand the fallacy in this claim, we need only to look at how evolution stacks up against the three hallmarks of science that I outlined in chapter 2. Evolution clearly satisfies the first hallmark, which states that science seeks explanations for observed phenomena that rely solely on natural causes. It also clearly meets the second, which states that science progresses through the creation and testing of models. For example, the very idea of evolution won out over Aristotle's competing idea of species that never changed, and Darwin's theory won out over Lamarck's earlier model because it explained the observations so much more successfully. The objections from the opponents therefore usually revolve around the third hallmark, which states that a scientific model must make testable predictions that would lead us to revise or abandon the model if the predictions do not agree with observations.

In essence, the opponents claim that evolution is a matter of faith because it does not make testable predictions. *But it does.* For example, the modern theory of evolution, understood on a molecular level, predicts that diseases can and will evolve in response to medicines designed to combat them, a prediction borne out in the rapid way that many diseases acquire drug resistance. It also predicts that genetically similar species should respond to medicines in similar ways, a prediction confirmed by the fact that we can test many medicines in other primates and they do indeed have effects similar to those they have in humans. The theory of evolution also provides a road map that we can use to modify organisms through genetic engineering; in this sense, every genetically engineered grain of rice or corn represents a success of the predictive abilities of the theory of evolution.

In fact, even Darwin's original theory made testable predictions. For natural selection to be possible, Darwin had to assume that living organisms have some way of passing on their heritable traits from parent to offspring. So although he did not predict the existence of DNA per se, his theory clearly predicted that some type of mechanism had to exist to carry the hereditary information. Moreover, now that we understand DNA and its role in heredity, the theory of evolution predicts that closely related species should also be genetically similar, a prediction that has been confirmed in just the past few years by genome sequencing. For example, in the ordering of their base sequences, the DNA of humans and chimpanzees is 98.5 percent identical. Similarly, DNA studies show that primates are all more closely related to one another than to other animals, that animals are all more closely related to one another than they are to plants, that plants and animals together are more closely related to each other than to bacteria, and so on. These relationships are clearly expected according to the theory of evolution, and they would make no sense if we were incorrect about the mechanism by which mutations in DNA make possible natural selection.

Note that none of this makes any statement at all about whether a God or anyone else has had a guiding hand in evolution. Indeed, as you can see in the quotation at the beginning of this chapter, even Darwin himself thought he might be seeing God's hand in creation. Like Darwin and countless other scientists, you are free to believe in your religion and evolution at the same time. You're even free to believe that none of it is true, and that all the scientists who accept it are sadly misguided. But the fact is that these same scientists are using the theory of evolution to advance medicine, agriculture, ecology, and human knowledge of the biological universe. Whether you believe them or not, if you want your kids to grow up able to make similar contributions to our civilization, it is crucial that we teach evolution in school, and teach it well.

Acknowledgments

Writing this book provides me with a wonderful opportunity to thank some of the many people who have helped me develop the ideas about teaching that I've presented. Of course, it also means that I'm likely to forget to include a few key individuals, to whom I offer my sincere apologies. I'll go approximately in chronological order.

My teaching career began when I was in high school, during which time I taught swim lessons to both children and adults, and helped with younger kids in the school at Temple Beth Israel in San Diego; at the latter, I learned a great deal from the mentorship of Helene Schlaufman. My next and perhaps most important mentor for teaching was Anne Earlywine, who taught the grades 2–3 class (at Sunset View Elementary in San Diego) in which I worked as an aide during a year off from college, and in which I continued to volunteer for several more years.

During my undergraduate years, I learned a great deal more about teaching by working as a tutor for the OASIS learning center at the University of California, San Diego. Early in graduate school, I had great help from the professors for whom I worked as a teaching assistant, including Tom Ayres (who later became my PhD thesis advisor and worked with me in developing the Colorado Scale Model Solar System), George Dulk, J. Michael Shull, and Dick McCray. During the same period, dozens of parents (and kids!) from the San Diego area helped me improve a curriculum I created for a science-based summer school that I taught and directed with classroom space graciously provided at no cost by Point Loma Nazarene University.

Later in my graduate career, I began teaching for the University of Colorado's Honors Program and Young Scholars Program (a summer program for high school students), in which my key mentors were J. McKim Malville and Jack Kelso. Upon graduation, I began developing and teaching a new mathematics curriculum in quantitative reasoning at the University of Colorado, in which my ideas developed with the help of numerous others who worked with me; I'd especially like to acknowledge many valuable conversations about teaching with David Wilson, Hal Huntsman, and Marc Anderson.

And throughout most of my career, I've learned more than I can possibly acknowledge from the colleagues with whom I've developed educational programs and written books, especially Mark Voit, Megan Donahue, Nick Schneider, Bill Briggs, Cherilynn Morrow, and Jeff Goldstein. I hope all of these individuals — and the many more I haven't named here — will find that I've done justice to what they have taught me about teaching.

Finally, I'd like to add special thanks to the people who reviewed this manuscript in various stages: Debbie Brown-Biggs, Dr. Josh Colwell, Dr. James Cooney, Dr. Megan Donahue, Dr. Laura L. Duncan, John DiElsi, Dr. Richard Gelderman, Dr. Scott Hidreth, Dr. Susan Lederer, Mark Levy, Dr. Alan McCormack, Dr. Kevin McLin, Dr. Lauren Monowar-Jones, Michelle Shearer, Dr. Holly Travis, Patricia Tribe, Dr. David Wittman, and Dr. Jeffrey Writer.

Detailed List of Headings and Notes (with Page Numbers)

Figures and Tables

Index

About the Author

Jeffrey Bennett, winner of the 2013 American Institute of Physics Science Communication Award, holds a B.A. in Biophysics (University of California, San Diego) and an M.S. and Ph.D. in Astrophysics (University of Colorado). His extensive educational experience includes teaching at every level from preschool through graduate school, proposing and helping to develop the *Voyage* Scale Model Solar System on the National Mall in Washington, DC, creating the first broad-based curriculum for courses in quantitative reasoning, and serving two years as a Visiting Senior Scientist at NASA headquarters, where he helped create numerous programs designed to build stronger links between the research and education communities. He is the lead author of college textbooks in astronomy, astrobiology, mathematics, and statistics that together have sold more than 1 million copies, and of critically acclaimed books for the general public, including *Beyond UFOs* (Princeton University Press, 2008/2011), *Math for Life* (Big Kid Science, 2014), and *What Is Relativity?* (Columbia University Press, 2014). His five books for children were selected as the first set of books for NASA's new "Story Time From Space" program, for which they were launched to the International Space Station in January 2014. His personal web site is www.jeffreybennett.com.

Visit the Web Site

Although it's not an absolute promise, we hope to use the web site as a place where you can get updates and additional information, and post your own comments or suggestions relevant to the material in this book. Please visit it to see if you find it useful:

www.OnTeachingScience.com